Dark Places
Dark Times

Johnnie Johnson

For my dearest Fay

Mahal kita Iniibig kita

About the author

Since his retirement in 1988, Johnnie Johnson has written some thirty books, ranging from true crime and superstition to local history and the supernatural. Writing as Allen Makepeace, he has written two novels, one of which, *And Such Great Names as These*, was awarded the prize for 'best novel' by the National Association of Writers' Groups. He was a winner of the now defunct South East Arts Prose Prize and a finalist for the Fenner Brockway Peace Prize for Literature and the international Alpha to Omega Short Story Competition. This is his final book.

Acknowledgements

I must emphasise how much over the years I have relied on the professional experience of my friend, the author-publisher, David Arscott. Once again I am extremely grateful to him, not least for introducing me to David Johnston whose illustrations so enliven this text. Many thanks, gents!

Printed by 4Edge, Hockley, Essex SS5 4AD.

CONTENTS

Author's note:

Remember The Pickwick Papers and Mr Tupman? He's one of Mr Pickwick's colleagues and he's fallen in love with Mr Wardle's unmarried sister. Then here comes Joe, the Fat Boy, one of Mr Wardle's servants, who has spotted the romancing couple. He keeps his information to himself until he has a chance to speak to Mr Wardle's aged mother. Such a great piece of gossip, he thinks. He knows, of course, that the old lady will react with horror at any suggestion of her daughter engaging in an affair with a man. It's such a great story for the Fat Boy to relate and he admits, 'I wants to make your flesh creep.'

I am your Fat Boy and I have the same purpose. I want to make your flesh creep, and I hope that the following accounts will succeed in that intention . . .

Sawney Bean

I was a cannibal for twenty-five years. For the rest I have been a vegetarian.

George Bernard Shaw

The following story – and note my choice of the word 'story' rather than 'account'– has been told and retold down the years. Indeed it might have originated in the middle ages or even before that. It smacks of some old 'bogey man' tale, an invention not founded on truth but simply on the desire to thrill and chill its listeners. So I am uncertain of its historical origins. Is it just some made-up narrative to be told in front of the winter fire in some old peasant hut in the days before reading matter was available? Or must there always have been some basis in fact, some series of horrific events out of which have come the twisted truths of Scotland's past and its cannibals?

First let me just say something of Christie-cleke who was born, allegedly, in the mid-fourteenth century – there is some doubt about his very existence – and began his supposed career as a butcher. But times were hard and trade fell away but he seems to have been a shrewd fellow. He fell in with a band of scavengers who were suffering seriously from starvation and he had an answer to their problem. He cut up the corpse of a former member of the gang and prepared a much-appreciated meal. His companions' problems were solved and thereafter they sought out unsuspecting but appetising strangers for the larder. From now, they never went hungry. Christie became the leader of the gang, both strategist and presumably head chef. It is alleged that he gained his soubriquet for being skilled with a cleke, a hooked stick, with which he pulled his targets off their horses.

Eventually the terrifying company was wiped out by an armed force from Perth. So many were killed at this bloody confrontation though not Christie, cunning soul that he was. He escaped, changed his name, and went on to become a prosperous and respectable citizen. Really?

Then there was the story of a child, a girl aged twelve, who was arrested and charged with cannibalism. In court she made a spirited reply.

'Why do you thus rail at me as if I had done such an heinous offence contrary to the nature of. man?' she asked, sounding more like a sixth former from an elite establishment. 'I tell you that if you did eat it, you'd find how pleasant is the taste of man's flesh. None of you would forbear to eat.'

But pert comments have never been well received in court, especially from those who ought to know their station in life. They hanged her.

As for Christie-cleke, who might have been a mythical figure, he has never enjoyed the fearsome reputation of his possibly equally imaginary countryman, Sawney Bean.

But just imagine that Sawney Bean *did* live, that he was born in East Lothian, about eight or nine miles east of Edinburgh, some time, say, in the fourteenth century.

His parents made a scanty living, hedging and ditching but Sawney had no love for this kind of work and, perhaps in his late teens, he left home with an alleged witch named Black Agnes Douglas, the 'Black' suggesting either her dark hair or perhaps her vicious inclinations. A remarkable pair, they set up their seaside home in a cave at Bennane Head on the Galloway shore. At high tide each day the cave was inaccessible and for the twenty-five years they lived there, safe and dry, deep inside at the end of a tunnel said by some to be a mile long. Here they were shut away from the world, along with their growing brood, and emerged, so it seems, only to rob and slaughter hundreds of folk passing through this desolate land and to live off their flesh.

The Newgate Calendar reports, with its usual sober relish, 'In the night time they frequently threw legs and arms of the unhappy wretches they had murdered into the sea, at a great distance from their bloody habitation. The limbs were often cast up by the tide in several parts of the countryside.'

Over the years the Beans had a great number of children and grand-children – forty-eight, so it is said – but no outsiders were ever introduced to the family. All of them, every member, so it seems, shared the blood as well as the blood-lust of Sawney and Black Agnes. They had no sense of compassion for others. That they murdered so extravagantly did not trouble them. Love and conscience had no place in that ghastly cave. No-one whose path they crossed was ever identified, as no-one ever escaped once the ferocious gang attacked, perhaps half a dozen at a time or even, so it is claimed, by two on horseback. And did they really keep horses? In a cave? The number of the people these savages destroyed was never exactly known, but the suggestions are that in the twenty-five years they continued their butcheries, they had washed their hands in the blood of at least a thousand men, women and children.

And so it went on down the years, this grisly nightmare. Occasionally, people were paid to search the area but no-one ever came near to resolving the mystery of the missing many. The authorities, of course, had to appear to be seeking answers and, because there were always whispers, several people, both local and travellers, were questioned, and some innocents were taken up on the flimsiest suspicions and wrongfully hanged. There was an almost fevered willingness to do something, to capture somebody, anybody, to force by brutal means even a false confession and all the time Sawney and his blood-crazed brood of cannibals continued their killing. So many innocents were executed by the law but not one of them did other than proclaim his innocence, even at the last, with a rough rope around the neck, even at the gallows foot.

Then, quite unplanned, it was all ended. A wife and husband, sharing their one horse, he with the reins, she with her arms tightly round his waist, were coming home from a fair one evening when they were ambushed by Sawney's merciless wretches. They fell upon the couple in a most furious manner. The man, still on horseback, fought very bravely against them with sword and dagger but his wife was pulled down to the ground, perhaps by someone with a clete. The terrified woman was instantly murdered by some of Bean's womenfolk who cut her throat and started sucking her blood. Then they ripped open her belly, pulling out her entrails. Her husband continued this desperate fight, fearing the same fate as his wife. And it was at this point, and quite by chance for it was late in the evening, that twenty or thirty men who had also been at the fair came across the fray. The murderers fled. This was the first occasion that any one of Sawney Bean's many victims escaped.

But this time the victors identified the direction the shrieking mob had taken to escape. Immediately messengers were posted to Glasgow where the Provost was alerted and he in turn sent information to King James (which James is unclear) who, leading four hundred men, set out

to destroy the murderous creatures who had for so long terrorised that huge area of south-west Scotland. They were difficult to locate and the searchers ignored one great cave, flooded as it was by the tide at least once every day. It was absurd to imagine anyone living there. And then one morning, at low tide, the bloodhounds had a scent and set up such a howling at the mouth of the cave that the hunters knew that their search was nearing its conclusion. Into the dark of the cave the searchers went. Finally the pursuers, torches in hand, came to the great hall where their quarry hid below.

And it was horrifying.

It was a butcher's shop.

There was meat hanging, enough for a small army. Any manner of cuts that a man – or woman or child – might desire, hung there. Legs, arms, hands and feet of men, women and children hung from the walls and ceilings. And the barrels were full of chops, of kidneys, livers, brains, hearts, all pickled and salted. There might be a world of famine outside but inside this cave none would starve had he the taste for such meat. Men, women and children might starve out there in the great world. But here was abundance.

But, oh, the stench. The cave reeked from what hung there, all manner of hacked-off body parts. And thrown there. it seems almost at random, was a mass of money, both gold and silver, with necklaces, rings, swords, pistols, and a large quantity of clothing, both linen and woollen, all together in great heaps or hung up against the sides of the den.

Now the family was discovered and the awful truths about it were uncovered. Sawney's family, which had begun with only Black Agnes and him, now consisted of eight sons, six daughters, eighteen grandsons, and fourteen granddaughters, most of whom had been begotten incestuously. The astonished victors, their minds no doubt a-whirl at what they had discovered, took the cursed tribe back to the Edinburgh Tolbooth, from whence they went next day to nearby Leith, where they were all executed without legal process for they were not regarded as human. They were professed enemies of mankind. The men and boys had their privy-members cut off and thrown into the fire. Their hands and legs were severed and they were left to bleed to death. Black Agnes and her daughters and grandchildren, having been made to watch the men's punishment, were afterwards tied to stakes and burnt to death. Without a word of repentance.

Just a folk tale? Or is it some twisted version of the truth?

Witchcraft in Rye

Fillet of a fenny snake;
In the cauldron boil and bake;
Wool of bat and tongue of dog;
Adder's fork and blind-worm's sting;
Lizard's leg and owlet's wing;
For a charm of powerful trouble,
Like a hell-broth, boil and bubble.

Shakespeare's *Macbeth.*

It's a witches' incantation, isn't it? Makes the blood run cold when you think about it. Eye of newt? Lizard's leg? What kind of crazy concoction is this? Well, there are certainly people around the world today – as well as way back in Shakespeare's time and before – who still practise witchcraft. But do they really use these strange ingredients? Fenny snakes? And newts and toads? And think of the dog, the adder and the blind-worm and the owlet.

But worry not. A newt's eye is a real enough part of the creature's anatomy, but the witches were unlikely to have committed horrific tortures on newts or on any of the other animals mentioned in the spell. These were all doubtless ingredients in witches' spells, but in many cases they are simply the ancient names for certain herbs, flowers and plants. Perhaps in earlier times, wishing to add a degree of mystery and perhaps menace, those claiming magical powers added such fictitious details to their spells. So, as you'll remember, the victorious, battle-stained soldier Macbeth, making for home, chances upon some witches chorusing their magic spell. And pretty fearsome it all sounds until you know that the ingredients are not as described.

Translation: what was in the pot was not so grim and grisly as first announced.

Here's what the old girls were cooking up: eye of newt was mustard seed and toe of frog no more than buttercup. Wool of bat was simply holly leaves, and tongue of dog, like adder's fork, were merely plants. Different from the rest was the blind-worm. Okay, that's a genuine poisonous snake but I imagine that it was added to the fictitious brew by Shakespeare to give it a bit of a kick.

Now you can make a witch's brew yourself if you're so inclined! However, I seriously don't recommend that you actually ingest it. Legend has it, by the way, that witches were predisposed to picking up anything lying about so my advice to you, if you are of nervous disposition, is to scatter mustard seeds by your front door or around your bed. You'll be absolutely safe because witches are given to counting abandoned items over and over again. So a witch will never have time to get to you as she (or he!) will be too busy counting mustard seeds. I don't know about you but I fancy that the classic scene from Macbeth just wouldn't be the same if his characters spoke of boiling mustard seeds, buttercups and holly leaves.

Now to continue with a more serious tale about spells and witches and spirits being seemingly conjured up. That the following account is impossible to believe, that it seems totally fraudulent, is the reasons for its inclusion here. So bizarre, so absurd in 2021, are the events described here but they do emphasise how the world has changed in the last four hundred years. The witch trial at Rye in 1607 was astonishing and it took place in Shakespeare's time. Two suspected witches came before a civil court, presided over by the mayor, to consider the case. Had either woman 'consulted, covenanted with, entertained, fed or rewarded any evil or wicked spirit to or for any intent or purpose?' These were serious questions and the women were to answer further charges relating to the recent death of a former mayor.

But now to set the scene. In Lion Street in Rye were two adjoining houses where the curious events of the spring and summer of 1607 occurred. The houses were owned by Mrs Susanna Bennett, who shared the larger house with her daughter, Ann, and her wealthy son-in-law, George Taylor, described in legal documents as a 'gentleman'. Both Ann and her mother were known locally as 'healers,' using local herbs as medicines, with perhaps an occasional casting of spells, to cure minor ailments.

Mrs Bennett let out the ground and first floors of the smaller attached house to Roger Swapper, a sawyer, and his wife Susanna. One day, after the first mysterious happenings occurred, Susanna visited Ann Taylor with a story you and I should have immediately rejected, but matters were different in 1607. Today she might have been sent to a psychologist but at that time her claims were not in doubt.

According to Susanna, her first spirit-visitors came one spring night when she was in bed. There were two men, a young one called Richard, wearing a white surplice and an older man, Robert, in a white doublet and hose. They were with two young women, Catherine and Margery, also dressed in white. Oddly enough, Susanna had not been frightened by her mysterious visitors. Instructed by her spirit visitors to consult her neighbours, she told Ann Taylor of her experience and assured her that it was not a dream. She had been fully awake. After the spirits appeared on two subsequent occasions, Ann urged Susanna to ask them what they wanted instead of simply gaping at them.

One night, the Catherine-spirit appeared alone and tried to drag Susanna from her bed. She resisted and her arms were severely bruised. Then Catherine left but just before dawn all four spirits appeared. The bewildered woman asked, 'In the Name of the Father, Son and Holy Ghost, what would you have me to do?' And she might well have asked how these spirits got into the house when doors and windows were tight shut.

Catherine then told the bewildered woman that she must sow sage seeds in her garden. Later, Susanna called on Ann to tell her what the spirits had directed her to do. Ann seems not to have thought this a totally outlandish request and the two women set to work sowing seeds though they left off when Susanna felt ill. Why was she ill?

Another night one of the spirits told Susanna of a cache of gold and silver coins which was to be found at Weekes Green at nearby Playden. The following day Susanna went to Weekes Green where she met Richard, the young spirit, who led her through fields to a spot where he pointed out the location of what he claimed to be buried treasure. Then came a parade of figures. According to Richard, one female, dressed in green, was the Queen of the Fairies. Susanna was asked to kneel to her Highness but refused. The visions then disappeared and Susanna, feeling ill yet again struggled home.

In July 1607 the Taylors' daughter Elizabeth died. Had she been bewitched? The Taylors asked Susanna about this and she in turn then asked Richard on his next visit. There was no satisfactory answer to this question.

Then in September came the death of George, another Taylor child. Susanna went to the funeral where she claimed to have seen Richard in attendance. What next?

Over the next several weeks Susanna had more visions, outside and inside the house. She estimated that she had seen at least a thousand spirits. One day in Rye, Susanna saw Richard who spoke to her briefly. At other times, she experienced other visions: apparitions reflected in the windows of the house; a man's head; two ladies; a man drinking; death's heads.

Perhaps the last manifestation was the time when Susanna heard a loud stamping noise coming from the attic above her rooms. She ventured upstairs and entered the attic but once inside she was paralysed, unable to speak or move hand or foot. She remained in that position until her husband found her later in the day. This is the first mention of the husband. Did they not sleep together? He appears to have had no part in these events.

Now you may be saying to yourself 'What a load of tosh!' But then you weren't raised in these seventeenth century beliefs. Just cling on to the idea that scholarly folk did believe in ghosts and spirits and good and bad spells, For the most part, these were the strongly held beliefs of kings, queens, scholars, soldiers, people right across the social spectrum. So back to our tale.

Finally, the mayor of Rye took notice of the stories of these respectable folk whom he probably knew. And it might have been difficult for him to act as he did. Both women, Susanna and Ann, were charged with witchcraft. The trial in a civil court, presided over by the mayor, began in September 1607. And it rambled on for years. The two women were imprisoned in Rye's Ypres Tower, although Ann was released on bail of £100 (possibly equivalent to £200,000 today). Susanna, however, languished in the Tower. Finally both women were found guilty and sentenced to hang.

But afterwards there was a change of heart and in 1611 both were declared innocent. But why? New evidence? It's as unclear today as it probably was at the time.

So what really happened? Was it a series of japes played on a mentally ill neighbour? Had Ann Taylor, along with others, concocted the whole business? Was it all a grotesque pantomime? Had they entered the Swappers' bedroom by simply crossing from the attic in Mrs Bennett's house into the unleased top floor? But would Ann Taylor, having recently lost two children, have felt like continuing this cruel and complex deception?

Does it matter if it was all an elaborate hoax? What is more important is that the authorities believed the women to be dabbling in witchcraft. Had they been conjuring up these figures, they were asked? Were they really fairies, those emanations seen at Weekes Green? Apparitions seen in the glass? Suggestions of spirits capable of paralysing anyone? And they had asked for food and water, these spirits, and had been given them. And, so it was said, flowers, posies, left on window ledges had just disappeared, taken presumably by the spirits that the women had raised. Even though eventually found not guilty, in the minds of some people these women would always be guilty. But of what?

Matthew Hopkins,
the Witchfinder General

For first the Divels policie is great, in perswading many to come of their own accord to be tryed, perswading them their marks* are so close they shall not be found out, so as diverse have come 10 or 12 miles to be searched of their own accord, and hanged for their labour, (as one Meggs a Baker did, who lived within 7 Miles of Norwich, and was hanged at Norwich Assizes for witchcraft).

The Discovery of Witches, Matthew Hopkins 1647.

Of all times, it was during the Civil War when there was another internal enemy to contend with. It wasn't simply a matter of the Divine Right of Kings but something closer to home and to daily life. It was witches, a matter now become a frenetic concern. Witches bent on evil. Carrying out the work of the Devil. Accusations and executions. And how East Anglia suffered. Already there was bitter rivalry in that part of the world with some folk espousing the royalist cause and just as many were equally enthusiastic for the opposing side. As if that weren't enough to exercise people's minds.

At the beginning, in Essex, Matthew Hopkins, the self-styled Witchfinder General, and his leading accomplice, John Stearne, had investigated and had brought to court many they believed guilty of witchcraft and such folk were then sent on to the atrocious conditions of the forbidding Colchester Castle. Enough to sap anyone's spirit. But there were so many complaints about the misplaced zeal of the two inquisitors and their team of men and women that they were persuaded for their own good to move on to some other area. Essex had enough miseries without witch hunts.

Next, and almost immediately, the two zealots turned up in Suffolk with their small team. Here, they listened to accusations of ill-wishing, heard confessions of the most personal matters, pricked with needles and knives to discover any who did not bleed, considered information against neighbours implicated in pacts with the Devil. Such tales were told, some merely spiteful. At the lower end of the scale, there were childishly constructed accusations of the spoiling of beer or pies but some of them were

* *Witches' bodies were said to have distinguishing features: scars, blemishes, located in unusual parts of the body.*

more serious, the crippling of cattle or the ruining of crops. And the very worst, the word was out about people acting with murderous intent, of victims being cursed to death.

But when, in those past times, was death ever far away? Average life expectancy then was forty years, with over 12 per cent of all children dead in their first year. But now, these increasing fears of bewitchment led to a panic, a hysterical response to the very thought of witchcraft, just as there had been sixty-five years earlier in St Osyth in Essex and just as there would be in Bideford down in Devon thirty years later.

So numerous, however, were the feverish denunciations in Suffolk in 1645 that prisons and lock-ups were seriously overcrowded with the accused, the one-time 'curers' whose ministrations down the centuries had been welcomed; the old ladies passing on the folk-medicines they'd inherited from their parents; and those who'd pass on tips about lucky charms and others who would, with a gentle soothing of the udders, get the old cow a-milking again. Such folk were suspects now.

And the accusations and questioning doubts: who had raised these storms? Damaged these homes? Burnt these haystacks? And all out of wickedness and envy, wasn't it? And it must have seemed to some that God and Christ and all the saints had failed them. Where could people now turn to but to the magic makers?

As for those now often-friendless folk in crowded cells, being left for days without knowing precisely what was to happen to them: what about those poor wretches? After long hours of trying to keep up their courage, not knowing what was to happen to them, when at last they were questioned, they were already vulnerable to suggestions that they were guilty of consorting with the Devil and all manner of attendant wickedness.

And the interrogators knew what physical signs to look for. They'd been schooled throughout their lives to recognise Satan's signs. Their parents had told them, as had their grandparents and aunts and uncles. It only required Hopkins and Stearne to remind them to take such signs seriously and many old folk, particularly women, who had down the years been regarded as helpful 'cunning folk', were now revealed as the Devil's followers.

But why then did they confess to such devilish concerns? Perhaps it was the whole unexpected process of the so-called 'searchers', Hopkins's small team of men and women who were careful to search only members of their own sex. After first stripping the accused, they closely inspected all parts of the body. Wasn't that scarlet birthmark on the back significant? And that scaly skin on the left arm. What about that? Sure sign of the Devil. The bodies of several of the accused bore such distinctive features, inescapable proof that these were the teats on which the Devil's imps fed?

And all before they ever stepped into the court room, the prisoners were being readied. Probably the most effective way of breaking them down was to deprive them of sleep for days and days and then perhaps, wakened suddenly from a doze, they were forcibly 'walked' up and down for long periods. In the end – and we know this, for such measures have been used in certain countries in very recent years – a man or woman would say anything for a chance to escape to some blessed oblivion. Sleep deprivation causes great mental and physical strain. So some of these Suffolk folk confessed to all sorts of offences and on occasion even implicated other innocent souls, relatives, friends, anybody, provided they could bring their own dire situation to some kind of conclusion.

Despite the threatening presence of the Royalist army only half a day's march away, the first trial of witchcraft suspects took place on Tuesday 26 at Bury St Edmunds. On the following day, eighteen people received death sentences. Hopkins and Stearne and the rest of their team had been diligent in preparing people to face charges which in many cases would lead them to the scaffold.

There were several mentions of imps at the trial as everyone, accusers and accused, believed in the existence of such creatures, whether they appeared in the form of kittens or toads or snails or wasps. And we hear of a dog but 'with legs not so long as our finger . . . but his back as broad as two dogs, or broader.'

At their trial, Mary and Nathanial Bacon were accused of owning imps and sealing a pact with the Devil. And Jane Linstead is said to have 'freely confessed' to the ownership of three imps who sucked at her breasts regularly. She had even sent one of her imps to kill a neighbour's daughter.

It only required Hopkins and Stearne to remind the searchers to take such signs seriously and many of the 'cunning folk' now charged with being the Devil's followers began to believe in their own culpability.

Among the condemned was John Lowes, the vicar of Brandeston for fifty years, who admitted to having made a pact with the Devil, enabling him to raise a storm which caused a ship off Harwich to founder with all lives lost. This clergyman claimed he had six imps working for him and when the inquisitors looked for evidence, they found what was considered to be a teat on the top of his head and two under his tongue. It seemed undeniable that the 80-year-old Lowes was in league with the Devil. So here he was now, accused of witchcraft. So, simply to be doubly certain, they put him in the moat at Framlingham Castle to see if he would sink or swim. Well, he didn't drown, undeniable proof of his guilt, his accusers claimed. He was one of the eighteen hanged. On the same day, that day on which eighteen people were sentenced to death, a man and his wife confessed to having brewed beer which had caused several deaths. They had even, so they said, deliberately caused the death of their own grandchild. Another pair for the gallows.

After sentencing, all the condemned were kept overnight in a barn where they sang hymns and prayed and then, all save one, kept a vow of silence until they met their end the following morning. They were not outraged by this injustice. They seem to have accepted their fate as though it were thoroughly deserved.

And so, the two men, Hopkins, the self-styled Witchfinder General, and Stearne, his deputy, along with their helpers, continued what they announced as 'God's work.' The death toll at the Suffolk Summer Assize of 1645 finally ended up with sixty-eight condemned and no-one had been physically tortured. Mind games had persuaded these confessions. And they still do in certain countries.

What authority did Hopkins and Stern have to carry out their work? There is no evidence of their having been given authority by the government. It seems they simply set themselves up without consent. Regardless of their abilities, weren't they just like some cheap-jack company fresh on the market? What did they claim about themselves, save that they were willing to contest the Devil and all his works? But what right did they have in such a matter?

The mission that Hopkins and Stearne pursued came to a conclusion in 1647. They were responsible for much suffering. It is uncertain how many deaths but they were responsible for more people being executed for witchcraft than in the previous hundred years, and solely responsible for the increase in witch trials during those years.

If these two men were in the business simply to make money, as some have said, perhaps funds were drying up. But such an activity with a team to support could not be done without an income. There were grumbles about their charges though Hopkins stoutly defended himself against accusations that he and those with him were simply lining their pockets.

But, in any event, it could not have lasted much longer for in August 1647 Hopkins died of tuberculosis. He was twenty-seven-years old. How could such a young fellow have managed to rouse so many anxieties and convince so many people to follow his arguments? Or so many to admit that they were servants of Satan? Simple. They already believed in Δ19witchcraft. They simply needed to be persuaded that they were them-selves already corrupted.

As for Stearne, a member of the gentry, he simply went off to live as a farmer on his estate in Lawshall, near Bury St Edmunds. One wonders how, with his reputation, he was greeted as a member of the community. In any event, he survived there until his death in 1670.

The jury of today seems to have reached a verdict on Hopkins and Stearne. That they were either bullies or frauds seems to be the general conclusion. For my part, I do not believe that we have evidence either way.

Jack Sheppard,
an Artful Dodger

'I am the Sheppard, and all the Gaolers in the Town are my Flock,
and I cannot stir into the Country, but they are all at my Heels.'
The History of the Remarkable Life of Jack Sheppard, Daniel Defoe

Had he lived in our time I have no doubt that Jack Sheppard would have been a celebrity, just as he was for several months of his lifetime in early eighteenth century London. He could not but have failed to captivate great audiences watching him on Saturday night TV, this cheerful little criminal – not a murderer, you understand, but a small-time thief, a pick-pocket, a feller who, as he would have put it in his rich criminal cant, 'went out on the dob' (breaking and entering), cocking a snook at the world, as the saying went then as now. It was not his law-breaking that people came to admire but his wonderful skill in escaping from prison cells.

And he had the capacity to attract the admiration and the attention of those about him. His undistinguished thieving career lasted no more than a couple of years and he didn't, unlike an earlier character, Captain Blood, try to steal the crown jewels. He was a star, no doubt about it, but a shooting star – here but a few seconds and then gone for ever, leaving a memory of the brief magical trail he blazed. No, it was Jack Sheppard's way of blowing a raspberry at the authorities that was so engaging, and didn't they deserve having a raspberry blown at them? After all, they were upholding an outrageously ferocious punishment system which fell especially hard on those at the bottom of the ladder.

So where did it all begin? Pretty well in the home of the widowed Mrs Sheppard who was totally unable to support her young family even though only two of her four children had survived. She managed to send Jack to Mr Garrett's school which was in the Bishopsgate workhouse when he was six years of age. He seems to have been a willing pupil, a boy with some ability that might just enable him to rise out of the depressing possibilities awaiting most children in his situation. So, an apt youth, at the age of ten he went to work for a wool draper in the Strand where his employer taught him to read and write. After this, he was apprenticed to a carpenter in Drury Lane, signing a seven-year indenture in April, 1717. At this point, Jack, a bright, hard-working lad, looked to be destined for a better future.

He clearly had a compelling personality. He was quite small, perhaps 5'4", and of a light build. Even so, he was strong, this attractive looking young man with the large dark eyes and the ready smile. It's not surprising to learn that he took to frequenting the Black Lion in Drury Lane and perhaps it was here where he reached a turning point, for this particular pub was regularly frequented by criminals, including two who were to play some part in Jack's life. The first was Joseph 'Blueskin' Blake, a young mulatto already enlisted in the ranks of crime, and perhaps he spoke to Jack about a life of fun and excitement and sometimes with money to spare, more money than a man might ever earn as a carpenter. And it was here, too, that Jack first made the acquaintance of the notorious Jonathan Wild, an arch criminal, who was also a major police informer, a top man with people on both sides of the law following his advice. And then there was yet another influence on Jack's life. He met Elizabeth Lyon, a prostitute better known as Edgeworth Bess. And it was in such a company that Jack Sheppard suddenly realised that while it was all right being a respectable carpenter, it was so much more fun being a law-breaker. And weren't the rewards greater?

So Jack became a thief, although one must admit that it was not to be his best career choice, for he turned out to be quite ineffective as a 'dip' and not a particularly skilled breaking and entering man ('heaving a cough' never seemed to come easy to Jack). Along with 'Blueskin', for a brief time – a mere weekend – he became a highwayman, but the successful in this line always had horses. This must have dawned on Jack and his companion in the space of a mere forty-eight hours. The brutal truth is that Jack Sheppard had one great skill. In the time in which he plied his criminal trade – and I emphasise that this lasted a mere couple of years – his real successes came after he was taken prisoner. He was a poor lawbreaker but an outstanding prison escaper. That is why Jack Sheppard was known and so much admired.

Here then are some of the recorded highlights of the great escaper's short life:

25 July 1724 Yesterday one Shepheard, [sic] a notorious house-breaker, who lately made his escape from New-Prison . . .was committed to Newgate, having been re-taken by Jonathan Wild; he is charged with several burglaries, &c. (*The Daily Journal*)

14 August 1724 .[Sheppard convicted of burglary]

1 September 1724 Yesterday . . . a most surprising accident happen'd at Newgate . . . John Sheppard, the malefactor afore-mention'd, finding himself order'd for execution, and being provided of saws, files, and other implements, found an opportunity to cut off one of the great iron spikes over the door of the Condemn'd Hold, and being of a very slender body, got himself thro' into the Lodge, and from thence into the street, and so escap'd, assisted by his wife and another woman . . . He went off in his irons, which were hid by a night-gown, and he is suppos'd to have immediately taken coach . . . Other condemn'd prisoners intended to follow his example, but were prevented by a timely discovery. (*The Daily Journal*)

2 September 1724 We are certainly inform'd, that John Sheppard went off by water, at between seven and eight on Monday night last, at Black-Fryers-Stairs; the Waterman saw his irons under his night-gown, and was much terrified thereat. He landed him at the Horse-Ferry at Westminster, and for which he rewarded him with seven pence. (*The Daily Journal*)

4 September 1724
John Sheppard's Letter to Jack Ketch*

SIR,
I thank you for the favour you intended me this day: I am a Gentleman, and allow you to be the same, and I hope can forgive injuries . . . and to show that I am in charity, I am now drinking your health, and a Bon Repo [sic] . . . This night I am going upon a mansion for a supply; it's a stout fortification . . . but bars and chains are but trifling obstacles in the way of your Friend and Servant JOHN SHEPPARD. (*The Daily Journal*)

4 September 1724 [Joseph Ward and Anthony Upton were executed on this day. Sheppard had been destined to accompany them to the scaffold.]

11 September 1724 Yesterday, about noon, John Sheppard, the malefactor, who made his escape from the Condemn'd Hold of Newgate, on Monday the 31st of August, was apprehended and by the Officers and Turnkeys of that Prison, at Finchley, near Highgate, in company with one William Page, an apprentice to a butcher. The last patiently surrender'd, and Sheppard took to the hedges, where being discover'd, and pistols presented to his head, he begg'd them not to shoot him on the spot and submitted. There were found upon him two silver watches, a large knife, and a chisel, and a knife only upon his companion; they were both disguised in butchers blue frocks, and woollen aprons. Being brought to town, Sheppard was carried to Newgate, loaded with heavy irons, and put into the Condemn'd Hold, and chain'd. William Page was examined, and committed to Newgate, with orders to be doubled iron'd, and to be kept from Sheppard . . . and he was accordingly put into the Castle, and his friends are not permitted to see him. In the evening a Divine and several Gentlemen went into the Condemn'd Hold to Sheppard, who seem'd compos'd and chearful, and acknowledg'd the manner of his escape . . . He took a coach at the corner of the Old-Bailey, (along with a person, whom he refus'd to name) went to Black-Fryers-Stairs, and from thence by water to the Horse-Ferry, at Westminster, and came in the middle of the night to Clare-Market, where he met his companion, and there disguis'd themselves in the manner above-mention'd. From thence rambled to a relation of Page's, within seven miles

* 'Jack Ketch' was a generic term for the hangman.

of Northampton, where they were entertain'd a few days, and returned towards London. He has hinted, that he hath committed robberies since his escape, and denies that he was ever married to the woman [Elizabeth Lyon] who assisted him therein, and who is now in the Compter [a small prison in the City of London] for the same, declaring that he found her a common strumpet in Drury-Lane, and that she hath been the cause of all hismisfortunes and misery; he takes great pains to excuse his companion Page of being any ways privy to his crimes, whom he says only generously accompanied him after his escape; he hath promised to clear his conscience as this day, and to be more particular in his confessions . . . This morning a Gentleman goes to Windsor to procure an order or warrant for his speedy execution, and 'tis thought that the same will be on Monday next. (*The Daily Journal*)

14 September 1724 Sheppard . . . is visited by the Reverend Mr Wagstaff and the Reverend Mr Hawkins in the Condemn'd Hold; and yesterday he was carried up to the Chapel in Newgate, for the first time, since his being retaken, where was a very great concourse of people to see him. He hath confess'd, that on Tuesday the 8th instant, two days before he was taken, he came from Finchly into Bishopsgate-street, and drank at several publick houses; and in the evening came into Smithfield, went thro' Christ's Hospital, and pick'd two people's pockets in the Cloysters, and from thence pass'd under Newgate, down the Old-Bailey, and into Fleet-street; where taking notice of Mr Martin's, a watchmaker's shop, against St Bride's Church, and only a little boy to look after it, he meditated to robb the same, and perfected his villainous design in the manner following, viz. He first fix'd a nail-piercer into the post of the door, next fasten'd the knocker thereto with a pack thread, and then cut out a pane of glass, and took three silver watches out of the shop window; the boy seeing him take the watches, but could not get out to pursue him, by reason of his subtle contrivance; one whereof he pawn'd for a guinea and an half, and the two others were taken upon him at Finchly. He denies that his fellow-traveller Page was privy to this robbery; but if we are rightly instructed, Mr Page was accompanying him all that night, and was aiding and assisting in this fact; and, just before it was executed, came into the shop, and ask'd the boy some trifling questions, the better to observe the inside, &c. This, with some other circumstances, will, as we are told, be prov'd against Page: if so, in all probability he may accompany his friend Sheppard (according to our witty

brother) in his Cart and Two. On Saturday night the Keepers found a small file conceal'd in a Bible, which was lent him for his preparations. (*The Daily Journal*)

17 September 1724 Yesterday morning the Keepers of Newgate, going into the Condemn'd-Hold to Sheppard, found two files, a chissel, and a hammer, hid in the bottom of a matter chair, with which he had begun to file his irons, who when he perceiv'd his last effort to escape thus discovered and frustrated, his wicked and obdurate heart began to relent, and he shed abundance of tears; he was carried up to an apartment call'd the Castle, in the body of the Gaol, a place of equal, if not superiour strength to the Condemn'd-Hold, and there chain'd down to the floor. (*The Daily Journal*)

21 September 1724 Sheppard confesses that he and Blueskin were the ones who robbed Mr Pargiter on Hampstead Road on 20th July, for which Francis and Benjamin Brightwell were tried and acquitted – the weight of which charge sate so heavy upon the spirits of the first [i.e. Francis Brightwell], that it broke his heart, and he died in a week after the trial. (*The Daily Journal*) 22 September 1724 We are now assured, that it must be proved in a regular and judicial way, that he [*i.e. Sheppard*] is the same person who was so convicted, and escaped, before a fresh order can be made for his execution [so Sheppard is to be tried again at the next Sessions]. (*The Daily Journal*)

3 October 1724 Joseph Blake, alias Blueskin, with two others, is appre-hended by Jonathan Wild and taken to Newgate. (*The Daily Journal*)

5 October 1724 [Blueskin is committed to Newgate], being charged upon the oath of William Field, a noted evidence [his accomplice in robbing Mr Kneebone]. This Blueskin was formerly himself an evidence against Junks alias Levee, Flood, and Oakey, who were executed at Tyburn for robbing the Honourable William Yonge, Esq and Colonel Cope near Hamstead. (*The Daily Journal*)

10 October 1724 Sheppard's brother is transported to the Plantations [either Ireland or Florida]. Sheppard makes repeated attempts to escape during the month.

17 October 1724   On Wednesday last the Sessions began at the Old-Baily, when Joseph Blake, alias Blueskin (lately taken by Mr Jonathan Wild, and charged as an accomplice of Shephard, in the felony, for which he was condemn'd) was, among others, brought down from Newgate to the Old-Baily to be arraign'd, who, as he was talking with Mr Wild in the Yard, on 5 October just under the leads of the Court, he, on a sudden, took out of his pocket a little knife, and catching hold of Jonathan round the neck, attempted to cut his throat, and had it not been for a thick muslin stock that stopp'd and blunted the knife, it is thought he had done it before the Turnkey could turn himself about to take him off; he wounded him much, but happily missed his windpipe, but the wound being sow'd up, and able surgeons attending him, it is not doubted but that he will do again: the desperate villain triumphed afterwards in what he had done, lamented that he had not done it more effectual, and bitterly swore that then he should have died with satisfaction; nay, he wished he could have cut off his head, and thrown it over the wall into the Yard among the rable [sic. rabble]; so that honest Jonathan stands a fine chance among those rogues. (*The Weekly Journal or Saturday's-Post*)

17 October 1724   [Sheppard makes yet another successful escape from Newgate.]

29 October 1724   [Sheppard's mother goes to St James's Palace] to beg a pardon for her unfortunate son. (*The Daily Journal*)

30 October 1724   John Sheppard's LETTER to Joseph Blake, alias Blewskin, under sentence of death in Newgate.

Dear Joe I would come and give thee an Act of Grace, if I thought thee worthy. I am living, thou art dying, and Jonathan recovers; curse on thy little dull clasp knife; must I be plagu'd to finish what you so clumsily begun? had I wrought with such impliments? well, comfort thy self, a couple of kicks, a shrug, a wry neck, and a piss'd pair of breeches will make thee snug and easy. But if thou art still a man, show thyself such, step forth, bilk the prigs, and return to thy dear friend, John Sheppard. (*The Daily Journal*)

2 November 1724   [Sheppard is captured.]

3 November 1724 Yesterday several Noblemen and persons of distinction went to Newgate to see the famous John Sheppard . . .Two persons are appointed to watch him night and day. During this period of freedom, Sheppard made no real attempt to lie low. He managed one successful break-in and took enough money to dress elegantly in a black silk suit, with a diamond ring and a fine wig. He was finally captured while very drunk in the company of his two mistresses. (*The Daily Journal*)

4 November 1724 JUST PUBLISHED Eronania or the heinous Crime of Self-Defilement . . . On this crime in single persons, married, widowers, women-haters, or Molles . . . Of a certain person of quality who made his servant privy to this crime, and cut his tongue out that he shou'd not tell . . . Also, The History of the surprizing Life and Adventures of John Sheppard, and A Print of John Sheppard, with his Fetlocks and Handcuffs on, chain'd to the Floor in the Castle. (*The Daily Journal*)

9 November 1724 [Blueskin Blake is executed.]

10 November 1724 Yesterday petitions were deliver'd to several of the Nobility, on the behalf of John Sheppard the famous thief, house-breaker, and goal-breaker, beseeching them to intercede with his Majesty for his being transported beyond sea. (*The Daily Journal*)

11 November 1724 Yesterday morning, between ten and eleven, the notorious John Sheppard was convey'd in a hackney-coach from Newgate to Westminster, being handcuff'd and fetter'd, and guarded by a great number of Constables, &c. from Temple-Bar. In Westminster-Hall, his handcuffs were taken off; and being brought before the Court of King's-Bench, the Record of his conviction for burglary and felony at the Sessions in the Old-Baily, was read, and he making no objections, Mr Attorney-General mov'd that his execution might be speedy, and a Rule of Court made for Friday next. Sheppard address'd himself to the Bench, earnestly beseeching the Judges to intercede with his Majesty for mercy, and desired a copy of a petition he had sent to the King, might be read, which was comply'd with; but being ask'd how he came to repeat his crimes after his escapes, pleaded youth and ignorance, and withal his necessities; saying he was afraid of every child and dog that look'd at him, as being closely pursued; and had no opportunity to obtain his bread in an honest way, and

had fully determin'd to have left the Kingdom the Monday after he was retaken in Drury-Lane: He was told, the only thing to entitle him to his Majesty's Clemency, would be his making an ingenious discovery of those who abetted and assisted him in his last escape; he averr'd, that he had not the least assistance from any persons, but God Almighty, and that he had already named all his accomplices in robberies, who were either in custody or beyond sea, whither he would be glad to be sent himself. He was reprimanded for prophaning the name of God. Mr Justice Powis, after taking notice of the number and heinousness of his crimes, and giving him admonitions suitable to his sad circumstances, awarded sentence of death against him, and a Rule of Court was order'd for his execution on Monday next. He told the Court, that if they would let his handcuffs be put on, he, by his art, would take them off before their faces. He was remanded back to Newgate, thro' the most numerous crowds of people that ever was seen in London; and Westminster-Hall has not been so crowded in the memory of man. A Constable who attended, had his leg broke; and many other persons were hurt and wounded at Westminster-Hall Gate. (*The Daily Journal*)

13 November 1724   The Constables and Headboroughs of the Liberty of Westminster, &c. have orders to be out to preserve the peace on Monday next, when Sheppard is to be executed; and the Sheriffs have also order'd an extraordinary number of their officers to guard him to Tyburn, he is to be carried thither in his handcuffs and fetters. Last night Joseph Blake alias Blueskin, was buried from Chick-lane at St Andrew's Parish in Holborn. (*The Daily Journal*)

14 November 1724   Yesterday morning an eminent painter came into the Condemn'd Hold, and took a draught [i.e. drawing] of the famous John Sheppard. (*The Daily Journal*)

17 November 1724   Yesterday morning, about nine of the clock, the famous John Sheppard was carried up from the Condemn'd Hold to the Chapel in Newgate, where having heard prayers and received the Holy Sacrament, he was brought down again to the Press-Yard between ten and eleven, when Mr Watson came in the name of the sheriffs to demand his body; Mr Perry and Mr Reuse, after taking the proper receipt, deliver'd the same: Mr Watson told the prisoner, that he must put him on a pair of handcuffs for his security; he vehemently resisted the same, flying into the

greatest passion, and endeavour'd to beat the Officers; upon searching him, they found a penknife conceal'd about his cloaths, with which 'tis apprehended, he design'd to have cut the ropes, and attempted to escape out of the car. Never was such a concourse of people ever seen in Holborn, and the places leading to Tyburn. When he arrived at the Tree, he sent for Mr Applebee, a printer, into the cart, and in the view of several thousands of people, deliver'd to him a printed pamphlet, Entitled, a Narrative of all the Robberies and Escapes of John Sheppard, giving an exact Description of all his Robberies and Escapes, together with the wonderful Manner of his Escape from the Castle in Newgate, and of the Methods he took afterward...

N.B. The said Narrative is now publish'd by John Applebee, Printer, in Black-Fryers; and sold by the Booksellers of London and Westminster. (*The Daily Journal*)

5 December 1724 On Saturday last . . . at the Theatre in Drury-Lane, was a new entertainment call'd Harlequin Shepherd, which was dismiss'd with a universal hiss. And, indeed, if Shepherd had been as wretched, and as silly a rogue in the world, as the ingenious and witty Managers have made him upon the stage, the lower gentry, who attended him to Tyburn, wou'd never have pittied him when he was hang'd. (*The Weekly Journal or Saturday's Post*).

10 December 1724 [Page is convicted of robbery to the value of 4s. and 10d and assisting Sheppard.] Catherine Manone was fined six Nobles and ordered four months' imprisonment for receiving stolen goods from Sheppard. Elizabeth Lyon, alias Sheppard, alias Edgeworth Bess who had been many weeks confined in the Compter for assisting him in his escape . . .was discharg'd without bail. (*The Daily Journal*)

20 February 1725 Monday about 5 in the evening, the well-known Mr Jon. Wild was taken up at his house in the Old-Baily, and being caried before Sir John Fryar, was by him committed to Newgate. The particulars of his accusation are as yet uncertain, but we hear that very great bail has been refus'd, which occasions various speculations, some being apprehensive of the loss of his intelligence and protection, by his being oblig'd to travel, and others entertaining the more dismal opinion, that he'll leave the world in his own way, and die in his shoes. (*The Weekly Journal, or British Gazetteer*)

3 April 1725   Edgeworth Bess, alias Elizabeth Lyon, alias Elizabeth Sheppard, an accomplice of the late John Sheppard executed at Tyburn, and who assisted him in several of his escapes, was last week committed to Tothill-Fields Bridewell, for seducing a shopkeeper's son to go a-thieving with her. (*The Weekly Journal, or British Gazetteer*)

24 May 1725 Jonathan Wild, a London underworld figure who operated on both sides of the law, posing as a public-spirited crime fighter entitled the 'Thief-Taker General', was executed on this date. (*The Weekly Journal, or British Gazetteer*)

Postscript
Daniel Defoe and John Apledee, his publisher, planned to retrieve and revive Sheppard after the requisite fifteen minutes on the gallows. In rare cases, hanged men and women had survived execution. Unfortunately, the lurching, heaving mob surged forward to pull on Sheppard's legs, intending to ensure him a swift death. The crowd was too dense for Defoe's plan to be effected. Jack Sheppard was buried that night in the graveyard of St Martin-in-the-Fields.

Oh, 'tis my dear husband's head

'In the meantime the head had been discovered, and the circumstance
of a murder having been committed being undoubted, every means was
taken to secure the discovery of its perpetrators.'
The Newgate Calendar

Catherine Hayes, born in Birmingham in 1690, was a girl of wilful
temperament who, at the age of fifteen, fell out with her impoverished
parents and ran away from home. In the course of her journey, she fell in
with some soldiers, officers according to some sources, who persuaded her to

accompany them to Worcestershire. So,
fancy free, and having guaranteed
meals probably for the first time in her
life, off she went with them. Let there
be little doubt that she was highly
entertained by her new friends and
doubtless in turn she offered equally
entertaining responses as far as the
soldiery was concerned.

After a while we find Catherine
living in in Warwickshire, employed by
a respectable farmer, Mr Hayes, whose
twenty-year-old son, John, was much
taken with her. It seemed a
genuine love match, the kind of affair
that might be described as 'love at first
sight' and John, keen beyond measure, prevailed upon his not totally
enthusiastic father to give him a property valued at about £26 a year which
would allow him to marry Catherine. And so, Catherine Hayes' world, in
the space of only a dozen months or so, was completely transformed, And
in time, others' lives would be transformed.

Six years or so of marriage and tired perhaps of the rural Midlands,
Catherine persuaded her husband to move to London. There they took a
quite large house, part of which they let as lodgings. At the same time John
opened a business as a coal merchant and chandler (selling candles). It was
a highly successful business and Hayes added to this by setting up as a
money-lender cum pawnbroker.

As for Catherine, with time she turned out to be not the most agreeable of women, acquiring a reputation for being both unpleasant and argumentative, constantly haranguing her neighbours. It is difficult to tell what she felt about her husband because sometimes she spoke of him very fondly and at other times she would complain about how unsatisfactory he was. And there were other tales to the effect that he was abusive towards her. On one occasion – or perhaps even more frequently than that – Catherine was heard to say that she would think it no more a sin to murder him than to kill a dog. But it might have been said with a laugh and a shake of the head.

Mightn't it?

They moved house at one point to the Tyburn Road (now Oxford Street), at that time almost on the outskirts of the city and business still flourished. It was about this time, in late 1725, that twenty-one-year old Thomas Billings came to lodge with them. There was a story that this young man was Catherine's son, conceived by her when she was only fourteen and put out then for adoption. How was it that they were able after all these years to team up together? This is not clear from the records. Some might have suggested it was simply a story put about when her wickedness came to light a few months later. Just as there were claims that she slept with the young fellow on a regular basis. Could that possibly be true? No doubt about it, said some. You could believe anything about that shameless hussy. But in the end it seems that it was true that the young man was the son of John and Catherine. But why so long apart? And how had they found each other? And now here they were, so suddenly under the same roof. And in the same bed.

Catherine's unpleasant behaviour towards her neighbours, and perhaps even customers, continued unabated. On one occasion, when her husband was away from home on business, her behaviour was so excessively gross that not only did the neighbours quarrel with her but a fight broke out. And, of course, when Hayes came back the whole unseemly business was reported to him. What shame he must have felt, this man, brought up in a respectable household. Not that his behaviour was ever entirely perfect but it seems that, whatever his temper, nothing was ever demonstrated in public. But that wife of his . . . oh dear. What a harridan she was.

More arguments. More lectures from him. More loud responses from her. She talks to young Billings, complains about John. Fed up with him. And it must have been about now that she reached her decision to do away with her husband, and she had an ally in Billings. It was about this time Thomas Ward came to town and found lodgings with the Hayes.

Now, work this out. Ward seems not to have met Catherine previously but apparently, in a brief space of time, she was sleeping with him. Can her husband have known that she had two lovers in the house? Or did he not care? And Ward, within only a few weeks of his arrival, was also informed of her wish to kill her husband. And like young Billings, he fell in line. Yes, he'd help and presumably he felt quite justified when Catherine told him that John was an atheist who had stopped her going to church. And he had, she confided, already murdered two of his own children probably at birth. It is impossible to know the truth of this. Was he such a monster? Or was she the only monster in the house?

Catherine, by the way, had also mentioned the £1500 which she'd receive from his will and she promised both of her young lovers that this would be used to reward them should she ever need to call on them for help. Astonishing. A woman planning to rid herself of her husband finds that her two lodgers, whom she has known for only a relatively brief period, are quite willing to support her plan.

Soon the opportunity presented itself. One evening, Catherine with Billings and John Hayes were drinking in a pub. They had all drunk considerable quantities. Hayes, unaware of what was planned for him, bragged about how much he had drunk and how much more he intended to drink. His smiling, laughing, joking, back-slapping companions, offered him another glass and poured him another drink, told him another good joke and poured yet another. And so it went on.

They finally went home, where John Hayes, still much encouraged by the others, continued drinking, before finally staggering to bed. Now was the time. Billings, urged by Catherine, went with her and found the hatchet and on their return to the bedroom where Hayes was sleeping his last sleep, he struck a blow so violent that the skull was fractured. Ward then took the hatchet from Billings and gave their victim two more blows. Raucous, elated perhaps, they all three made such a noise that another lodger went to complain to Catherine that the noise was waking her husband and child. Catherine explained that they'd been having a little party but it was all over now. Uncharacteristically, on this occasion, Catherine offered an apology to her tenant.

Now came the matter of disposing of the body. Catherine suggested cutting off the head in order to make difficult any attempt at identification if the body were ever found. They had a knife. Catherine's role was to hold a pail to collect the blood so that the floor wouldn't be stained. Then there was some discussion about the head. Should they boil it? It might be good to do so as boiling would cause the flesh to fall off the skull. It couldn't then be identified. But instead they decided to throw it in the Thames, assuming that it would be carried off miles away by the tide.

As they were taking the head downstairs, the lodger again came out of her room and called down to them. Such terrible noise, she complained. Exhilaration, one supposes, sheer excitement. Just saying goodbye to her husband, Catherine explained. She knew it was late but it was important to see him off. He was likely to be gone for quite a while, and that was absolutely true.

So then, the neighbour satisfied with the excuse, off went the two young men ready to dispose of the skull. The skull, however, proved to be something of a problem. They'd carried it up to the dock expecting it to be taken away by the tide but they hadn't reckoned closely enough that it was an ebb tide. A lighterman, out in the river, saw something being thrown in the water and, presumably curious and perhaps wanting to relieve the boredom of his lonely night-time labours, he decided to investigate. And being a conscientious soul, and possibly a fellow hardened to whatever the river might turn up, he dutifully took along his find to the local authorities.

Back at the lodgings there was still work to do. There was the rest of the corpse to deal with. They decided, first of all to put it in a box and bury it but as with the best laid plans of mice and men, they found the box too small. The only alternative, as there appeared to be no other more suitable container, was to dismember the body, a task which had to be done straightaway because headless corpses cannot be left hanging about the house. They cannot be simply tucked up in a cupboard or a coalhouse (as has been done at times but with little success). Now they set about their work in the hope that the whole ghastly business would soon be over. So much for vain hopes, even though they managed to cut up the body, there was still too much of it for the box. Finally they wrapped the parts in a blanket and took them off to a pond in Marylebone.

It was really a quite fruitless night's work. The head, rescued within hours by the lighterman, made its way to the local magistrates who ordered it to be cleaned and insisted that the hair be combed After this it was placed on a pole for display in the churchyard of St Margaret's Westminster where it proved to be a real attraction to huge crowds, among whom were several who claimed to recognise it but even so, no-one was confident enough to say it belonged to John Hayes. After four days' exposure the head was taken to a chemist who put it in a large glass vessel filled with spirit.

Of course, there was increasing talk among those who knew the Hayes family. Suspicions were aroused. Funny we've not seen your hubby lately, they were saying. And as days and weeks passed, the queries continued, the gossip never ending. Understandably, with fingers constantly pointed at her and snide catcalls hurled after her and her two young companions, life was becoming uncomfortable.

Even so, some people managed to talk to Catherine, asking where John was because he'd not been seen for several weeks. She, of course, had a story ready, saying that he was away on secret business. She confided that 'some time ago he happened to have a dispute with a man, and from angry words they came to violent blows so that Mr Hayes killed him.' The wife of the deceased had, according to Catherine, made up some cock-and-bull tale that John had promised to pay her a certain annual allowance. As he couldn't afford to pay and as the bereaved woman had now reported the killing of her husband to the authorities, he had gone to Portugal. He was trying to resolve the matter from there and would be home again soon. Not a very convincing tale, and apparently some of Catherine's explanations differed in detail from others. Inevitably, someone approached the magistrates about the very curious disappearance of John Hayes.

The head was brought out of storage again and, upon close inspection, it was decided that it was undoubtedly the incomplete version of John Hayes. Catherine along with Ward and Billings were taken in for further investigation.

At this stage, on the first day of their enquiries, the trio stood up well to searching questioning. None of them had any idea about the matter, each of them denying any knowledge of a murder. For their part, the magistrates were clearly uncertain about the explanations they had been offered and consequently they examined the trio again the following day. This time, when Catherine was before the magistrates, she asked might she see the head.

Accordingly she was taken to the surgeon's house. He brought out the head in its glass case. 'It is my dear husband's head,' Catherine wailed, holding the glass and weeping. Mr Westbrook, the surgeon, asked the distressed woman if she would like to have the head taken out of the glass so that she might see it more closely. Oh yes, indeed, she had replied, and in no time she was holding the head, kissing it several times. Might she have a lock of dear John's hair, she asked, and Mr Westbrook obliged without demur. It was a quite convincing performance.

That same day Thomas Ward appeared before the magistrates who questioned him yet again but he strenuously denied all knowledge of what might have happened to Hayes. He was sent to Tothill Fields Bridewell in Westminster where almost on arrival he learned that Hayes' body had been found in the pond in Marylebone. For Ward, this changed matters. The game was up as far as he was concerned. Almost immediately he made a confession. Now, with the news already leaked out, as he was transferred to Newgate, he was under protective armed escort lest the mob attack him.

Catherine, hearing the news of the discovery of her late husband's body, arranged a meeting with Billings and urged him, her lover, her son, to make his confession. What a calculating woman. Of course, she had not killed her husband. She had not struck a blow. It was the two men. She was almost certain that she would not be found guilty. But nevertheless, she had been involved, hadn't she? So she must face trial along with the two men.

The jury was to find Catherine as guilty as the men. They and the authorities could recognise the prime mover in all of this.

Found guilty of Petty treason (the murder of her superior, viz. her husband) Catherine begged them not to burn her at the stake as the law demanded. But the law is the law. After conviction Ward, extremely penitent and devout, caught a fever in prison from which he died.

Catherine and Billings were executed at Tyburn on 9 May 1726. It was a dreadful day, which began with an attempted escape by two prisoners and some innocent deaths and serious injuries among the spectators. As ever, there were huge crowds. *The Weekly Journal* and *The London Journal* report what occurred: 'A little before the above-named criminals were turned off, John Map and Henry Vigus attempted to escape. The former having slipt off his halter and hand-strings, leaped out of the cart, and the latter had likewise got off his halter, but was prevented from getting out of the cart. Map was immediately seized, and they both submitted to the fate of their fellow-sufferers.'

But the day's excitements continued.

'The scaffolding broke down two or three times near the place of execution, by which much damage was done; five or six persons were either killed on the spot, or are since dead; and several persons had their legs and arms broken. (*London Journal*)

There is little doubt that many there found this day with its alarms and several executions quite wonderful free entertainment. Billings behaved with apparent sincerity, accepting his guilt and saying no punishment could make up for the crime for which he was to be executed. After execution he was hung in chains and placed on public display.

In Catherine's case, after taking communion, she was taken on a horse-drawn sledge to Tyburn. On arrival an iron chain was put round her body and this was fixed to a stake near the gallows. As was custom in cases of petty treason, she was to be burned. It was usual in these cases – as an act of mercy! – for the rope round her neck to be pulled by the executioner so that by the time the flames reached the stake the victim was already dead.

'The fuel being placed round her, and lighted with a torch, she begg'd for the sake of Jesus, to be strangled first: whereupon the Executioner drew tight the halter, but the flame coming to his hand in the space of a second, he let it go, when she gave three dreadful shrieks; but the flames taking her on all sides, she was heard no more; and the Executioner throwing a piece of timber into the Fire, it broke her skull, when her brains came plentifully out; and in about an hour more she was entirely reduced to ashes. She confess'd herself guilty in part of the murder of her husband Mr John Hayes, for which she beg'd God and the world pardon, and declar'd she repented herself heartily for being concern'd in it: She had a great confidence of a happy state, because she said she was charitable and just in her dealings. She own'd Billings to be her son, and that his true name was Thomas Hayes. She was somewhat confus'd in her thought, and dyed in the Communion of the Church of England. Thomas Billings was the same day hang'd in chains within 100 yards of the gallows.' (*Weekly Journal* or *The British Gazetteer*)

And the crowd drifted home, jubilant, laughing. All in all, it had been a great day out.

Dick Turpin, John Palmer and Harrison Ainsworth

We have highwaymen now: we call them muggers and car-jackers and we
don't sing ballads about them or eulogise them for their brave exploits.
From a review of John Sharpe's *Dick Turpin: The Myth of the
English Highway-man*

Dick Turpin? Why, I've known his name most of my life. I still recall vividly
the name of his horse: Black Bess. And didn't he ride her all the way from
London to York? And didn't he rob the rich and give to the poor? Ah yes,
he was a real folk hero, Dick Turpin, a romantic figure, all derring-do. And
his name and his reputa-tion resonate still.

But, and I'm reluctant to admit it, this hero of my childhood turns out
to be a bit of a disappointment. He was an Essex boy, a farmer's son, born
in Thackstead. He had some basic education and later he was apprenticed
to a butcher in White-chapel. But alas, he was a poor representative of his
family: unruly, disobedient, lazy and ill-mannered. Still, he completed his
apprenticeship and then married young a local girl, Elizabeth Millington.

Now marriage is often the making of a man. He suddenly recognises
that he has responsibilities; that he has to settle down; to mind his manners.

But it didn't quite work out this
way for Dick. There were stories
about his stealing cattle from
local farms. He'd cut up the
beasts and sold off joints,
chops, steaks or whatever cut
you might fancy and delivered
to you door.

But he didn't have the right
approach to this cattle-stealing
business and it's a small enough
area and talk gets about. You
can't stop the talk. And it was
heard and pondered over by a
couple of servants of a Mr
Giles who lived in Plaistow.
Their master had had a couple
of oxen taken and these two

servants went off to Turpin's place where they found a couple of oxen, dead and stripped of their hides. Of course, it was impossible to state that these were the beasts from Mr Giles's farm. But even so ... It all seemed to be adding up, that young Turpin was a wrong'un.

Next thing we hear is that Dick's turned his hand to highway robbery. And he's successful, too, making regular calls on stage coaches on the Essex highway. Along with that, he does a spot of equally successful breaking and entering.

But he's brought up sharp and it's all so pitiful. He'd shot a fowl on somebody or other's land and he's arrested and charged. You can't go round private property doing what you will. The law is there to support property owners with all its might. Of course, when they start looking for him he's nowhere to be found.

There's a warrant out for Dick's arrest but he escapes the attentions of the law. As the officers come in the house where he's lodged , so Dick's out of the back window and he's off and nobody can find him.

But then, he's on the run and he has no money. But people like Dick always have friends and he contacts one of them, asks him to visit his missus and ask her for money and she sends enough to last some weeks.

Next thing, we find him working with smugglers, presumably as a batsman, protecting the tubmen carrying whatever goods were being transported. For a time this was a lucrative operation for many. In fact this was the so-called golden age of smuggling. But while many made a great success of this enterprise, some were caught. As was Dick Turpin who lost a considerable amount of his profits.

What next for versatile Dick? Perhaps deer-rustling from the great Epping Forest and other parklands of the south. But somehow it just didn't work. Perhaps venison was too costly for most. The money just wasn't coming in. So what next? Breaking and entering, a trade Dick already had some experience of.

Dick and his friends planned their strategy. Knock at the door of a substantial property and when it opens, dash in mob-handed taking whoever was inside by surprise. It had to be a quick job, in and out, a case of picking up whatever looked saleable.

The first attack made by the gang was at the house of the elderly Mr Strype, owner of a chandler's shop at Watford. Easy. No difficulties. Mr Strype stood by calmly while Dick and his associates took everything of value they could find and they didn't hurt the old fellow.

Dick then told his gang of the next venture, robbing an old lady living in Loughton. There was apparently a huge sum of money, £800, in her house. So off to the old lady's place, knock at the door, charge in and blindfold the old girl and her maid. And just to make sure they don't make a sound or make a move, they tie them up and gag them.

So then, where's the money? And they put it to the old woman: 'Where is it?' Dick shouts at her. But she doesn't answer. 'I'll set you on fire if you don't say where the money is,' Dick snarls. But she's stubborn. She's not saying. It's her money and not theirs. She's not going to give them a penny. So now these grown men pick her up and place her on the fire and she tries to stick it out but she can't. How could she? At last she tells them where her savings are and Dick and his followers depart with £400, rather less than they hoped for but still a tidy sum. Easy business, especially when you have a go at old people.

Next call, some weeks later, they've eyed up a farmer near Barking. But this time no-one answers the door when they knock. Word must be about, newspapers carrying warnings about strangers in the night probably. Well, they're in no way deterred. They're safe enough out here in the country.

So they break down the door and overcome the farmer, his wife, his son-in-law, and the servant maid. They tie them up and off they go with more than £700. Turpin's over the moon. 'Aye, this will do,' he says, 'if it would always be so!'

They're cock-a-hoop, these boys. They always seem to be successful. So why stop now? They don't. Now they've got their eyes on the home of Mr Mason, the keeper of Epping Forest. So they made their plans, carefully. Everyone knows his task: feller minding the horses, door keeper, front and back look-out, inside operators. Everything is going so smoothly.

But then, disaster. Turpin's off to London for a few days. He's flush. Wants a spot of pleasure. All work and no play . . . he tells himself. But at the crucial time, with money in his pockets, he's out enjoying himself and he drinks too much, to such a degree, that he totally forgets the appointment at Mr Mason's place.

Still, the raid goes on in the absence of their leader. Once in the house, having employed the usual knock at the door tactic, they beat and kick Mason savagely. An old man in the house escapes attack and Mr Mason's daughter manages to escape the invaders by hiding in a pigsty.

After ransacking the downstairs, the robbers go upstairs, causing deliberate damage wherever they set foot. They agree, for no apparent reason and before leaving on their task, to break all of the furniture in Mason's house. Is it simply that he is the top man at Epping Forest? They break everything that falls in their way, and finally make off taking £180 in cash.

Back to London they went, meeting Dick, and giving him, as their leader, his share even though he had taken no part in their latest depredations.

The next job took place on 11 January, 1735. Turpin and five of his companions went to the home of a wealthy farmer at Charlton in Kent. They arrived sometime between seven and eight in the evening and did the usual knock-and-dash-in as soon as the door opened. Mr Saunders was found in the parlour, with his wife and friends, playing cards. Their visitors warned them not to put up any resistance in which case they'd come to no harm. Some of the gang stood over the owners and their guests while the remainder, accompanied by Mr Saunders, searched upstairs, breaking open the bureau, cupboards and closets, and stealing about a hundred pounds. The robbery continued systematically and finally, their work complete, finding mince pies and bottles of wine, the robbers set to, toasting each other. Another triumph.

But they couldn't stay for ever enjoying themselves. Eventually, off the gang went, presumably noisily, pleased at yet another success, but not before making it clear that if any of those present – or indeed if any of their family members not now present – dared to sound the alarm or later advertise the marks of the stolen plate, they would receive another visit and be murdered.

Turpin's men are tireless. And they seem to have such good luck with their takings. And nowhere are there any descriptions of them. The division of the plunder having taken place, they go on 18 January to the house of Mr Sheldon, near Croydon, arriving there about seven in the evening. In the yard, they see a light in the stable, where they find the coachman attending his horses. They tie him up and go outside to find Mr Sheldon in the yard. They force him to take then inside the house where they steal eleven guineas along with valuable jewels and plate.

They had two jobs arranged for 4 February. One was near Stanmore, at the home of Mr Lawrence, of Edgware. They arrived at the house at about seven o'clock. Before going inside they met a shepherd boy whom they terrified by threatening to shoot him were he to make a noise. They removed his garters and used them to tie his hands. Then he was to lead then to the front door and call out to whoever answered it. Again he was warned that if he made one false move they would hurt him. But when the boy reached the door he was too terrified to speak. So one of the intruders knocked and was granted immediate entry along with his companions.

Mr Lawrence and one of his servants had cloths thrown over their faces. The boy was taken into another room and asked what fire arms were in the house. There was only old gun, he told them, and when they found it, one of the gang members dismantled it.

They then tied up Mr Lawrence and the servant, making them sit next to the boy. Turpin searched the old gentleman, taking from him a guinea and some silver. He was not totally satisfied with the take so far and he forced the old man to take them upstairs. Here they broke open a closet, stealing some money and plate, but it was still not sufficient to satisfy them. At this point, Mr Lawrence was threatened with savage consequences if he did not produce some worthwhile return. One of the gang took a kettle of water from the fire, and threw it over the old fellow, but fortunately it was not hot enough to scald him.

Meanwhile, one of the maidservants, who had been churning butter in the dairy, was found by one of the gang who forced her to go up to one of the bedrooms, where he raped her.

After an hour or so the house had been robbed of all the gang could carry. They then locked the family and servants in the parlour, threw the key to the house in the garden, and off they went to London with their plunder.

At last, as a consequence of this particular robbery, there was a proclamation issued for the arrest of the offenders, promising a pardon to any one of them who would give full information about Turpin and his accomplices. There was also a promise of a reward of fifty pounds on conviction. But there was no result. The Turpin gang continued their brutal robberies.

On 7 February, six of the gang assembled at the White Bear Inn, in Drury Lane, where they planned to robbing the house of Mr Francis, a farmer near Marylebone. When they arrived they found a servant in the cow-house. They tied him up, threatening him with death if he made any noise. Another servant was tied up in the stable.

At this point Mr Francis arrived home to have pistols pointed him. He would die, he was told, if he dared to resist. Having tied up Mr Francis and leaving him in the stable with the servants, the gang entered the house, tying up Mrs. Francis, her daughter, and the maidservant, and then they beat them. The house was rifled. The take included a silver tankard, a Charles I medal, a gold watch, several gold rings, a considerable sum of money, and a variety of valuable linen and other effects, which the gang took to London.

Now, there was a reward of a hundred pounds for the apprehension of the offenders. This time two of them were taken into custody, tried, convicted on the evidence of an accomplice, and hanged in chains. The gang dissolved. Dick went into the country. But not to retire.

On a journey towards Cambridge, Dick met a man, well dressed, and well mounted: chance of a good return from this little fop. He looked just the sort of fellow Dick favoured meeting. Holding out his pistol towards the gentleman, Dick demanded his money but, as it turned out, Dick, by chance, had met a fellow highwayman, Tom King, who did not deliver anything,

These two men soon struck the bargain. They worked together and committed a great number of robberies; so many that no public-house would receive them as guests. But lodgings? Where could they stay? Well, in Epping Forest which Dick knew well, they found a large cave, well hidden by a thicket of bushes and brambles. From here, between the King's Oak and the Loughton Road, they were able to live and stable their two horses and from this vantage point, they could watch for traffic on the road.

The two men conducted several robberies from here. It was said at the time that they robbed so many people that even the poor pedlars along the road, carried firearms for their defence. Turpin's wife, at this time, supplied them with necessities and on occasion spent the night in the cave.

One day, the pair saw two young women taking fourteen pounds for a sale of corn. Turpin decided to relieve them of the money. King, however, objected. He didn't feel it right to rob a couple of girls, pretty ones at that, but Turpin insisted and the girls were robbed.

On the way home the following day, they stopped a Mr Bradele, from London, who was riding in a four-wheeled carriage with his children. They took the gentleman's watch, money and an old mourning ring. This time Dick and Tom agreed to return the ring to Mr Bradele who said it was of great sentimental value.

As they had readily parted with the ring, Mr Bradele asked them how much he must give for the watch. King asked Dick's opinion. 'What say you? Here seems to be a good honest fellow. Shall we let him have the watch?'

Dick replied, 'Do as you please,' on which King said to the gentleman, 'You must pay six guineas for it: we'll never sell it for more, though the watch should be worth six and thirty.' The gentleman promised that the money should be left at The Dial, in Birchin Lane.

On 4 May, 1737, Dick committed murder – possibly though not certainly his first – and a £100 reward was offered for his capture. Thomas Morris, a servant of Mr Thompson, one of the keepers of Epping Forest, accompanied by a pedlar, had set off to catch him. When Dick saw the two men approaching his 'home', Morris carrying a gun, Dick wondered if they were poachers and called out that there were there were no hares thereabouts.

'No,' Morris replied, 'but I have found a Turpin.'

He pointed his pistol at Dick ordering him to surrender. But Turpin, seemingly unmoved, replied in a friendly enough manner, smiling, casual. And as he spoke, he edged away, backwards, till he could pick up his own gun. He shot the slow-witted Morris dead and the pedlar ran off terrified. Of course, the murder was reported at the highest level. Dick Turpin was already wanted in connection with several major instances of law breaking. And now, murder. What had happened was reported to the authorities who issued the following proclamation: 'It having been represented to the King, that Richard Turpin did, on Wednesday, the 4th of May last, barbarously murder Thomas Morris, servant to Henry Thompson, one of the keepers of Epping Forest, and commit other notorious felonies and robberies, near London, his Majesty is pleased to promise his most gracious pardon to any of his accomplices, and a reward of £200 to any person or persons that shall discover him, so that he may be apprehended and convicted.

'Turpin was born at Thackstead, in Essex, is about thirty, by trade a butcher, about five feet nine inches high, very much marked with the small-pox, his cheekbones broad, his face thinner towards the bottom; his visage short, pretty upright, and broad about the shoulders.'

Dick instantly beat a hasty retreat from the area, with his former companion, Tom King. He also sent a letter to his wife Elizabeth, asking her to meet him at The Eight Bells in Old Hatfield. The couple met there and then occurred one of those curious mishappenings which so many of us experience in our lives. Soon after their arrival they had met a butcher, to whom Dick owed five pounds.

No, he didn't dash off, this butcher. He didn't go looking for someone in authority to help him arrest this now celebrated villain. What immediately concerned this gentleman was the five-pounds debt. 'Come on, Turpin,' he called out, broadcasting the notorious surname. 'I know you have money now and if you will pay me, it will be of great service.'

Dick makes an excuse, tells the man that Elizabeth, his wife, is in the next room, which is true; that she has money; and that he'll get the money from her to pay him immediately.

Does Dick trust the butcher? Does the butcher trust Dick?

Off goes Dick into the next room and now the butcher starts to tell others in the bar with a few nods, some winks and a whispered hint or two that the person he's been talking to is none other than Dick Turpin. He implies that that they could take him into custody but only after he receives the money Dick owes him. But Dick's a wise old bird. He knows what's going on. He's been on the look-out for untrustworthy fellers for many years now. After five minutes, there's no Dick Turpin returning with the cash. And he's not in the next room though Elizabeth is still there, sitting next to the open window where the curtain blows gently and the sound of a horse's hooves can be heard gradually fading in the distance.

Weeks later, Dick found King and another man named Potter, who had recently teamed up with them. There were more plans and so off they went towards London. The only event in this journey was when they neared The Green Man, in Epping Forest. Here they overtook a Mr Major on a very fine horse. Turpin's horse seemed on its last legs and the owner of the other horse could not resist the exchange of horses that Dick proposed.

This robbery was committed on a Saturday evening but Mr Major had handbills printed immediately. Then came a message to the landlord of The Green Man, that Mr Major's horse had been left at The Red Lion in Whitechapel. Preparations were made. A message had arrived saying somebody was going to pick up the horse. Late the next night, Tom King's brother turned up to collect the horse and was immediately arrested. His protestations of innocence were in fact believed by his interrogators. He was clearly not the actual robber and he would be immediately set free, he was told, if he said who was waiting for the animal.

He told of a man in a white duffel coat who would be waiting for him and the horse in Red Lion Street. Here, Tom King was arrested but not before he drew a pistol which failed to fire.

Turpin, in the shadows, was watching, and when he saw what had happened to King, he rode forward presumably to gather up his fellow-thief. King shouted out, presumably referring to the man who had him in custody, 'Shoot him or we are taken,' and at this point Dick fired but his shot hit Tom, who cried out, 'Dick, you have killed me.' At which point Dick fled the scene.

King, gravely wounded, lived another week and told the authorities where Dick would be found. From his death bed, he directed them to a house near Hackney Marsh.

Dick was no longer there but apparently he was sorely distressed that he had killed his most loyal associate. For a considerable time he hid in Epping Forest and had some near escapes from searchers. He was eventually captured by a constable and charged with horse theft, but he managed to absent himself from an appearance at the magistrates court. But it was close enough. He was too well known in this old stamping ground of his. He decided to a change of place and identity, arriving in Welton, Yorkshire, in the guise of John Palmer, Gentleman. From here he would from time to time go down to Lincolnshire to steal horses and sell them on.

Dick sometimes accompanied neighbouring gentlemen on hunting and shooting parties. One evening, returning from a shooting expedition, he shot a cock belonging to his landlord. Astonished, Mr Hall, a neighbour, said, 'You've done wrong shooting your landlord's cock,' to which Turpin replied that if the gentleman would stay while he loaded his gun, he would shoot him also.

Insulted in this fashion, Mr Hall informed the landlord of what had passed. It must have seemed a serious threat, not the kind of exchange to which country gentlemen were accustomed. Hall approached the local magistrates about the lout who had so threatened him and they called for this Mr Palmer to appear in court at Beverley. There, the magistrates demanded security for his good behaviour, the kind of demand to which he, being Dick, was not accustomed. The magistrates for their part committed him to the Bridewell.

Further enquiries revealed that this newcomer made frequent journeys into Lincolnshire and on his return he always seemed to have money. And anyway, he had all these horses, coming and going. Was he a horse-stealer? Could he be a highwayman?

The magistrates were not totally satisfied. But here he was in the Bridewell. He wasn't going anywhere and so the magistrates visited him. Who really was he? they asked him. Where had he previously lived? And what might be the precise nature of his business?

As you might expect of a man who had lived his kind of life, Dick gave a full resume of his past, his good reputation, his reliability. About two years ago he had lived at Long Sutton, in Lincolnshire, he told them. He had been a butcher but bad luck, particularly with a sheep deal, resulted in his falling into debt so had tried to make a fresh start in Yorkshire.

The magistrates were not happy with Mr Palmer's account, and lingering doubts persuaded them to enquire further. A letter was sent to Lincolnshire which resulted in a quick reply from a from a local magistrate. Yes, John Palmer was well known in the district, though he had never carried on any trade there. He had been accused of sheep-stealing and had been in custody but had made his escape. There were also suggestions that he had been guilty of sheep-stealing.

Now the magistrates removed him from the Bridewell and transferred him to York Castle prison. Whilst there, two further charges of horse stealing in Lincolnshire were levelled at him.

After he had been in the prison for four months, he wrote a letter to his brother in Essex:

Dear Brother,
York, Feb. 6, 1739.
I am sorry to acquaint you, that I am now under confinement in York Castle, for horse-stealing. If I could procure an evidence from London to give me a character, that would go a great way towards my being acquitted. I had not been long in this county before my being apprehended, so that it would pass off the readier. For Heaven's sake dear brother, do not neglect me, you will know what I mean, when I say,
I am yours,
John Palmer.

This letter never reached Dick's brother. It was returned, unopened, to the post office in Essex because the brother would not pay the postage on it. Then it was accidentally seen by Mr Smith, a school-master, who having taught Turpin to write, immediately knew his hand. He took the letter to a magistrate who opened it. This led to the discovery that the supposed John Palmer was the real Richard Turpin.

One is inclined to say, parenthetically, that the revelation in this letter is puzzling. The whole business of a man refusing his brother's letter does not convince, and how Mr Smith should recognise the handwriting of a former pupil who probably left school at the age of ten is difficult to accept.

The Essex magistrates then sent Mr Smith to York, where Dick was immediately identified as the notorious criminal.

Hearing that the notorious Turpin was a prisoner in York Castle, people flocked from all parts of the country to take a view of him.

When he was brought to trial, Dick Turpin was found guilty and convicted on two charges of horse theft, for which he was sentenced to death. There was no reference to his having killed Thomas Morris in Epping Forest.

Prior to his execution, Dick purchased a new fustian frock coat and a pair of pumps. He was determined that he would go out in style. On the day before the execution he hired five poor men, at ten shillings each, to follow the cart as mourners: and he gave hatbands and gloves to several other people. He also left a ring, and some other articles, to a married woman in Lincolnshire with whom he had been acquainted.

On the morning of the execution he was put into a cart and, followed by his mourners, brought to the place of execution. On his way there he bowed and waved to the spectators with an air of complete indifference.

When climbing the ladder to 'the fatal tree', his right leg trembled and he stamped it down as though afraid of betraying his fear. He talked with the executioner for thirty minutes or so and then, with the halter round his neck, did not wait. Instead, he threw himself off the ladder, dying very quickly. He wasn't going to wait to be strangled.

The corpse was brought to The Blue Boar, in Castle Gate, York, and the following morning it was buried in the yard of St. George's parish. The grave was dug remarkably deep, but notwithstanding the measures taken to secure it, the body was carried off about three o'clock on the following morning. But the word was out and the corpse was later found in a garden belonging to one of the surgeons of the city. The recovered body was then laid on a board and carried through the streets in a kind of grand procession after which they filled the coffin with unslaked lime and reburied it in the original grave.

I'll repeat the opening paragraph for convenience:

Dick Turpin? Why, I've known his name most of my life. I still recall vividly the name of his horse: Black Bess. And didn't he ride her all the way from London to York, a celebrated ride indeed? And didn't he rob the rich and give to the poor? Ah yes, he was a real folk hero, Dick Turpin, a romantic figure, all derring-do. And his name and his reputation resonate still.

Just to say that there never was a Black Bess nor was there ever such a long ride from London to York. And there's no record of Dick Turpin giving to the poor. In fact, some people say that you'd never have heard of Dick Turpin if, in the nineteenth century, Harrison Ainsworth hadn't somehow come across the name of a quite modestly important eighteenth century criminal and placed him as the hero in his novel Rookwood.

Oh yes, and the gravestone bears two names: Dick Turpin and John Palmer.

Them that ask no questions isn't told a lie

If you see the stable-door setting open wide;
If you see a tired horse lying down inside;
If your mother mends a coat cut about and tore;
If the lining's wet and warm – don't you ask no more !
A Smuggler's Song, Rudyard Kipling)

There is a myth that tells of a Merrie England, of some Golden Age when the English countryman, that Noble Savage, dwelt in peace and harmony with his neighbours. Perhaps in the great cities, the Londons, the Bristols, there was vice, corruption, brutality, but, so the story goes, in the pastures and sheepfolds, in the villages and market towns, the idyll was undisturbed. Not so. Not in any century. Yet the romantic gloss of the old tales remains. We hear of gallant highwaymen, though these were few. We learn of heroic pirates (naturally our own and not the dastardly French or Dutch) and, most romantic of all, daring smugglers. But none of these beliefs bear much scrutiny and all that is required to dispel the legend of smuggling is to recount the last days of Daniel Chater and William Galley, victims in 1748 of what must rank among the vilest murders in the calendar of crime.

For centuries a brisk smuggling trade operated between France and the south coast of England. It developed into a highly professional, greatly sophisticated commercial venture, employing thousands of people at different levels, from the young farm lads who loaded and lifted the incoming and outgoing goods to those who led teams of pack horses by hidden ways from one safe house to another, from barns to midnight churchyards. There were also the armed escorts, men with cutlasses and horse-pistols and heavy batons, all fit and ready to take on the military or the riding officers who might dare to hinder their progress. And, truth to tell, not all citizens wished the trade to end,for how else could they have cheap tea, spirits and tobacco?

Such operations, carried on all over the southern counties, could never have succeeded without an intelligence web to support them, and such systems could not operate without money to corrupt the forces of law. Out of this huge industry, massive fortunes were made. Small wonder then that the great and complex framework on which smuggling depended was held in place by the most ruthless treatment of any who might seek to bring it down. This great criminal conspiracy was sustained by a merciless violence.

The murders of Chater and Galley, both of them in their sixties, were supreme examples of the smugglers at their worst. But it was these murders that were to break the Hawkhurst gang, the leading group among the loose confederation of smugglers across southern England.

These cruel atrocities coincided with the belated determination on the part of the authorities to bring the smugglers to book, for they had become far too powerful. In 1745 Parliament had commissioned a report into 'the most infamous practice of smuggling', for it appeared that the smugglers were now a law unto themselves. 'The smuglers [sic] will, one time or another, if not prevented, be the ruin of this kingdom.' At last it was recognised that the general peace of the land was endangered by bands of men who ignored the law and who might destroy the country.

In August 1747, only months before the murders, a correspondent in Horsham wrote, 'The outlawed and other smugglers in this and neighbouring Counties are so numerous and desperate that the inhabitants are in continual fear of the mischiefs which these horrid wretches not only threaten but actually perpetrate all round the Countryside.' Even so, some of the smugglers were regarded by many as local heroes; they were cult figures; they were famous, bold; they defied authority.

For example, they carried out an audacious plan in the autumn of 1747. On 4 October, men from the Hawkhurst gang, led by Thomas Kingsmill, met in Charlton Forest near Goodwood to concoct a scheme with a group of Dorset and Hampshire smugglers. They would break into the Customs House at Poole where some of *their* property was now being kept.

Two days later at eleven o'clock at night, after a second meeting at Rowlands Castle, thirty smugglers mounted guard in the area leading to the Customs House at Poole while another thirty, armed with axes and crow-bars, broke in. Imagine the nerve of it! They smashed the locks, wrenched off the bolts, hammered down the doors and made off with thirty hundredweight of tea valued then at five hundred pounds. It was rightfully theirs, they claimed. The tea and thirty-nine casks of brandy and rum which they had, weeks earlier, bought in Guernsey, had been seized at sea by a revenue ship on its way to the Dorset coast and lodged in the Customs House. But it wasn't really the customs men's property. How dare the customs service take it from them? Their mission accomplished, their audacious raid successfully completed, the men rode off triumphantly, each carrying five 27lb bags of tea.

Later on that morning many villages along the way turned out to greet the gang of mounted rascals as they passed, to wave and cheer them as they rode unhindered along the road. And it was at Fordingbridge, where they paused for breakfast and adulation, that Jack Diamond looked into the crowd and spotted the shoemaker Daniel Chater, a man he had worked with on the harvest some time past. Diamond shook the old man by the hand and gave him a small bag of tea. It was the first innocent step towards Chater's murder.

By the time the local authorities had roused themselves there was no sign of the smugglers but their coup echoed throughout the south. The government might make noises about the smuggling trade, about its pernicious effects, but it seemed as deep-rooted as ever, quite beyond control. And local people were tight-lipped, many of them grudging towards the authorities, others mindful that if they told what they knew they would suffer, for the smuggling gangs showed little mercy to those who passed on information about them.

Nevertheless, the authorities went about their business in the hope that something might emerge. And it did. Daniel Chater did not keep quiet about the bag of tea he had been given by Jack Diamond. Perhaps he bragged that he knew one of the great men, said that he was an acquaintance of one of those who had been to Poole. Even the dissolute great attract admiration.

But by February of the following year Jack Diamond had been arrested and lay in Chichester gaol. Whether he was there as a result of Chater's boasting and blabbing is unclear. After all, there was a reward of £500 on the head of each man who had broken into the Customs House, so perhaps this had led to Diamond's arrest.

Customs service officers had called on Chater. They had heard that he had spoken to Diamond at Fordingbridge in the company of the other smugglers, had been told that he had received a packet of the contraband tea. That being so, Chater was told, he was required to identify Diamond formally and then to swear before a magistrate that the smuggler had been carrying tea and had been armed. He was told that some later time he might be required to appear in court as a witness.

Chater had not known that it might come to this. He had never been prepared for such an eventuality, to swear the identity of the lawbreaker. He was aware of the possible consequences of giving information of this nature and we can imagine his reluctance to play the part asked of him. But what were the alternatives? He would be prosecuted, might even be sent to jail. He would be safe enough, Chater was reassured. He would have the backing of the law. He would be given protection. But he must have known that he could be a marked man.

The laxness of those who wished to use Chater as a prosecution witness in a major case of organised crime, their sheer casual attitude, is astonishing. Witness protection was paramount, and past experience ought to have been enough to warn those responsible that Daniel Chater could be in very real danger. As it was, Chater set out on the biting cold morning of Sunday 14 February, protected by one armed man, an equally aged, minor customs official, William Galley, with no previous experience of protecting a witness. Perhaps had these two men, who were to meet such horrific deaths, taken care to plan their journey they might not have fallen into the clutches of such wicked people as they did. But they did not know the precise route, and this ignorance led them quite by chance across the paths of their murderers.

The plan was that they should travel to Stanstead in the west of Sussex and there hand over a document to Major William Battine, a magistrate and surveyor general of customs for Sussex. But at Havant they were lost. Stanstead? In an age when few travelled far they probably asked directions several times and possibly received as many differing answers. But Rowlands Castle seemed a reasonable proposition and, wrapped up in their greatcoats, with an icy wind blowing, they made their miserable way. At the New Inn at Leigh they stopped off for a drink to warm their bones.

Perhaps the warmth of the pub cheered their spirits for Chater shows the important letter he is carrying to other customers. And Galley, perhaps not wishing to be outdone, may emphasise his significant role in looking after a man who is likely to be a star witness in an important forthcoming trial. They cannot help chattering, either of them, and then they bid farewell to their audience and continue their cruel and bitter winter journey.

Sometime after midday it is time for another halt, for they have been on their way for several hours and are yet again chilled to the bone. At Rowlands Castle they stop off at the White Hart and call for a tot of rum. Would that they had never called here. Would that they had never bragged about their mission to the widow, Elizabeth Payne, who has the licence here. They talk and she listens, and then they tell her that it is time for them to be off. But no, says the Widow Payne. They cannot leave, not yet: their horses are in the stable, they are told, and the ostler has just gone off with the key. He'll be back shortly, she says, so why not have another drink?

What else can they do? So they charge their glasses once more. And as they drink and await the return of the ostler, more customers, local men, come in. They join the two travellers, drink with them, talk about this important business they are on. Then Galley is unhappy, wonders if they aren't giving too much away, wonders if Chater is not talking just that bit too much, and why one man, Edmund Richards, has actually drawn a loaded pistol and pointed it at the drinkers, calling out, 'Whoever discovers anything that passes at this house today, I will blow his brains out.' The other customers are now told to drink up and leave. What can this mean? But along comes the Widow Payne, telling them all to cheer up and have another drink.

Out in the yard where he has gone to relieve himself, Galley meets one of those who have been drinking with them for the last hour or so. This is William Jackson of Westbourne. They have words. Galley says that he thinks that the witness is being interfered with and he pulls his warrant card out of his pocket. He is acting 'in the King's name,' he says. He is a King's officer, he tells Jackson. But Galley has no authority here. Perhaps he is already drunk. 'You a King's officer?' Jackson shouts at him. 'I'll make a King's officer of you. For a quatern of gin I'll serve you so again!' And back to the bar they go, staggering cheerfully.

Certainly an hour or so later both Galley and Chater are dead drunk and are carried off to bed. The letter that Chater has flourished so proudly is taken out of his pocket and destroyed.

Down in the taproom, those whom the Widow Payne so cunningly summoned earlier in the afternoon now discuss what they are to do with the two men asleep upstairs. They are dangerous company, smugglers all of them, and vicious too. William Jackson, the worst of characters, mistrusted even by those he works with, sits along alongside Edmund Richards, 'a notorious wicked fellow'. And there is also 'Little Harry' Sheerman and William Carter, as well as 'Little Sam' Downer, William Steele and John Raiss. They are discussing desperate measures. They are agreed that these men cannot be allowed to live. They are at one in that.

Yet, remember, an Act of Indemnity has been passed by the government. This act makes smugglers vulnerable to informers. Anyone, any smuggler, even one in custody, can, if he names accomplices, receive a pardon and a reward for all his past offences. The gang in the taproom know what their immediate intentions are but they do not know that, within the year, two of those at the table will name names, will betray the others sitting there.

Now all are agreed on everything but how to dispose of the two fellows sleeping off the afternoon's rum intake. Should they be instantly murdered? Steel suggests that they should get rid of them and throw the bodies down a local well, but that proposal is rejected. It is too close to home, the others are saying. What about keeping them permanently locked up? But that is impractical. The wives of Jackson and Carter have turned up and have felt at liberty to offer their own considered opinion on how the matter should be determined. 'Hang the dogs,' they urge their menfolk, 'for they came here to hang us.'

Eventually it was determined that they needed to be taken away from Rowlands Castle, as far away as possible. And so now, swathed in long mufflers and wearing heavy greatcoats, six of the group prepare their horses. Only John Raiss stays behind, as he has no horse.

Jackson and the others go to the room where Chater and Galley are still asleep. They are aroused by shouts, punches, whips which cut into their backs. Jackson raises his boot and draws his spur across the foreheads of both befuddled men. Still feeling the effects of the rum they drank earlier, the two wretched souls stagger out of the bedroom, go down to the taproom and are pushed out into the freezing air of early evening. Blows rain down on them. They are punched, the two old men. The heavily weighted ends of whip handles fall on their old shoulders. They are kicked and cursed and sneered at. They are already bewildered and frightened, these two men who had set off as innocents only that morning. No one says that they wept, but they surely did. There is no indication that they cried out for mercy, but there can be no doubt that they did.

Of course, their attackers are themselves drunk and they encourage each other in their brutality. Later, during the night, the effects of alcohol will wear off, but their ill-treatment will not lessen. Through the long hours of the night and into the following two days they will demonstrate not the least ounce of human sympathy. What they perpetrate cannot be excused as a consequence of too much drink. Not any one of this depraved group had even a moment's reflection that what was happening was beyond the frontier of human cruelty.

The two terrified captives are now placed up on one horse. Their ankles are tied under the horse's belly. And they are tied to each other by the legs. And now off they set towards Finchdean, with Jackson's voice calling out as they leave the White Hart yard, 'Whip the dogs! Cut them, slash them, damn them!'

So they make a slow trail across the frost-hard roadway, the gang members taking it in turn to follow Jackson's vicious injunctions. And who can stop them? Who can even know what they do in this empty, wooded, winter-dark countryside? Who can call out at the sight of the terrified victims, whimpering, flinching, striving to escape the blows? What sorts of men are these who cannot feel the slightest pity?

When they pass Woodhouse Ashes, the shoemaker and the customs official fall from the horse's back and their captors now suspend them beneath the animal's belly but then, tiring of this sport, they untie the two and then set them up once more on the horse's back and give them another beating for their pains. And Galley's coat, torn now from the blows of the whips, is taken off his back. He will feel the blows even more sharply now. And the cold. But let him not call out in pain as they pass through Finchdean. Let him not dare. Neither of them must make a noise now and the pistols are out and levelled at them. Later they slip from the horse again and once more find themselves upside down, their bound heels in the air, their heads trailing on the ground.

Now they are transferred. Galley is shoved up onto Steel's mount, sitting behind the rider, and Chater is placed similarly behind 'Little Sam'. But this arrangement does not save them. They are still beaten with the heavy whip handles. When they reach Lady Holt Park, Galley slips to the ground. In his pain the stricken man begs them to do away with him. He can bear this no longer. But they ignore his pleas and lift him up once more behind Steel. Yet again, as they cross Harting Down, Galley falls off the horse, and this time he is slung over Richards' horse and held in place by Carter and Jackson. Galley pleads with them again. 'For God's sake, shoot me through the head,' he shouts. But his captors laugh and Jackson squeezes the old man's genitals.

It is past midnight now and they've trailed along these roads and lanes and downland paths for the last six hours. They have called at only one house, an old friend's place, where they ask if they can stay for a while, but he sizes up the matter, sees the two captives, divines what it is that they intend, and turns them away.

Shortly after this in Conduit Lane, Galley slips sideways off the horse, calling out that he is falling. 'Fall and be damned,' 'Little Harry' Sheerman tells him, pushing him.

They get down to lift him from the ground but he is lifeless. So what now? Again, they lift him up, laying him across the saddle and the journey is resumed. They are making for Rake. Here at The Red Lion, the owner, William Scardefield, very unwillingly lets them in. He sees Chater, 'whose face was a gore of blood, many of his teeth beat out, his eyes swelled and one almost destroyed,' and beyond him, what may be a corpse. They have been in a fight with the Customs men, Scardefield is told. Some of their men have been killed and others wounded. They explain that somehow they have taken a prisoner or a witness and Scardefield wonders what they intend to do with him. He fears the worst but agrees to allow them to put the man in a hut while Galley's body is hidden temporarily in the brewhouse. After some time for further discussion and a drink, Galley's body is once more thrown across the horse's back. Scardefield leads the party to Harting Combe, a mile away where, in woodland and by lantern light, the body is buried by Carter, Downer and Steele.

Then through the hours from dawn until late at night the gang sit drinking in the Red Lion, pondering their next move. From time to time they check that Chater is still in the hut, but how can he not be? He is shackled to a post. That does not save him from their taunts, their threats, their kicks. They have not softened in their view of the helpless old man. Occasionally they give him food, but he vomits over himself, a hapless victim. Over the hours, not one of the gang has considered if what they are doing can in any way be justified.

But Chater is a problem. Not their exclusive problem, they tell themselves. After all, Jack Diamond is a Chichester man. This whole business is about him. They have done their share, these Hampshire men. Why not bring in the Sussex men? And so Jackson and 'Little Harry' Sherman go off to Trotton with Chater in tow, still being beaten with whips across the face and neck as they go along. They have gone to seek out an old smuggling rogue, Richard Mills. He will understand the problem. And he does. 'Major', for that is how he is known, locks the prisoner in a lean-to shed where normally he dries out turf for fuel. Here, on the freezing Monday night, Chater, exhausted and afraid, is placed on a pile of turf and chained to a beam. From time to time, 'Major' Mills comes in to taunt him as an informer, telling him that he will not live long. And 'Little Harry' and 'Little Sam' stand guard and add to the jeers and the blows.

Several of the gang return to their homes in the course of the Tuesday, fearful perhaps that their absence might arouse suspicion, but on the next day they make their way back to The Red Lion, this time with John Raiss. Here they are to meet 'Major' Mills on the Wednesday evening.

At this gathering are several Chichester men: John Cobby, William Hammond, Benjamin Tapner and Thomas Stringer; Daniel Perryer of Norton, 'Major' Mills and his sons, Richard and John, and, from Selborne, Thomas Willis.

What should they do? How should they kill him? Should they load a gun and level it at Chater's head and then tie a piece of string to the trigger. Then they could all pull on the string together. That would make them equally guilty. They would not then inform on each other. But that would mean the game was over, and there is no doubt that they were enjoying the game, the suffering, the power. At least it was agreed that the Sussex men should have the responsibility for getting rid of Chater.

'We have done our parts and you shall do yours,' Jackson told them. It was decided that Chater should be thrown down Harris's Well at Lady Holt Park. After all, the well was dry and never used. The body could lie there for ever and no one would ever suspect it.

The gang now returned to Trotton, where Chater still lay lonely in the lean-to. Tapner looked down at the helpless man and lunged forward with his clasp knife and cut him across the eyes and nose 'so that he almost cut both his eyes out and the gristle of his nose quite through'. But that was not enough for Tapner who then slashed him across the forehead. 'This knife shall be his butcher,' he shouted, but Mills was rather more cautious. It was his house after all. 'Pray don't murder him here. Carry him somewhere else before you do it.'

At the well, after another ride in the dark, Tapner placed a short cord round Chater's neck. No long drop for him, no sharp, sudden breaking of the neck. He would strangle slowly. He was made to clamber over the protective fence and pushed towards the well. The rope was tied to the fence and the feverishly frightened old man was pushed over, though, because of the shortness of the rope, only his legs dangled in the well. And for the next quarter of an hour, the victim of Stringer, Cobby and Hammond was at times either half-sitting or half-standing or suspended upside down by the ankles over the well. Then, at last, they let him go, headfirst. Even so, the still fearful old man did not die. They could hear him sobbing and groaning at the bottom of the well and they threw down two wooden gate posts and then large flints until eventually they silenced him. Chater's suffering had lasted from the Sunday afternoon until the early hours of Thursday.

For several months after, no one knew what had happened to either of the two missing men. There might well have been strong suspicions but as to who was responsible for their disappearance there was not the slightest hint. The gang must have felt very safe, for who would dare to report them?

As for the prosecution of Diamond, without the vital witness how could it be expected to prosper? Even the offer of further reward failed to produce the merest whisper until, quite out of the blue, there came an anonymous letter. Addressed to 'a Person of Distinction', it purported to come from 'one of the persons who had been a witness to some of the transactions of this bloody tragedy, though he was no way concerned in the murder'. It remains unknown who wrote the letter, but it contained vital information as to Galley's burial place. There is also an alternative account that Galley's body was found by chance by a gentleman out hunting.

The body was found buried in an almost standing position, still wearing boots, gloves, waistcoat and breeches. What struck those who dug it up was that the hands appeared to be covering the eyes. There were suggestions that Galley had not been dead when he was put in the ground. Rather, it was thought that he had been deeply unconscious when he was buried and that later he'd come to and had made some effort to struggle from his grave.

Then in September 1748 came another whisper, another breakthrough, leading this time to William Steele. Just a reminder: this is the William Steele who on Sunday afternoon at the White Hart had unsuccessfully proposed getting rid of Chater and Galley straightaway by killing them and dropping them down a well; the same Steele who was present at all the discussions at the Red Lion and at Mills's house at Trotton; the same man who with two others buried Galley's tortured frame. And, taken into custody, he recalled the Act of Indemnity and offered at once to tell the authorities what had happened and who exactly had been involved.

Then John Raiss came forward. One of the Hampshire men, he had played little part in the murder of Galley but he had played a significant role in the murder of Chater. He too offered the authorities all he could.

Now Chater's body was retrieved, 'a rope about his neck, his eyes appeared to have been cut or picked out of his head . . . They got his body out of the well with only one leg on'.

By October William Hammond and John Cobby were lodged in Horsham gaol, and the following month Benjamin Tapner was placed under arrest, he too charged with murder. Over the months others, including the two most vicious torturers, Jackson and Carter, were arrested. On 17 January 1749, at a Special Assize at Chichester, Mr Justice Foster handed down sentences of death on the eleven men standing in leg irons in the dock: Tapner, Cobbye and Hammond were named as principals in the murder of Daniel Chater; William Jackson and William Carter as principals in the murder of William Galley. These men were sentenced to be hanged and later gibbeted. 'Major' Mills and his son Richard were to suffer hanging but were not to be gibbeted. They were all to be executed the following day and so, on their return to gaol from court, five of them were measured for the chains and straps that they would wear on the gibbet after the tarring of their corpses. Within two hours of learning of his fate Jackson was dead, as a consequence, it is said, of fright.

At two o'clock on the afternoon of 18 January, with guards and dragoons in attendance, the six men due to hang in Chichester were marched through the town and up the Midhurst road to the Broyle. They climbed up onto a long waggon placed under the gallows which had cost £42 to erect, a sum that the corporation of Chichester would ultimately recover from the Exchequer.

Tapner, Hammond, Cobby and Carter took the opportunity to address the dense crowd, forgiving everyone, even the informants. 'Major' Mills and his son were less forgiving, refusing even at this stage to accept their guilt.

A letter from 'a Chichester correspondent', dated 20 January 1749, described the occasion: 'Young Mills talk't very narrowly and said we shall have a very jolly Hang of it and at the place of execution he said it was very hard to be refused a pint of beer which he had asked for. The father would have smok'd from the Gaol to the gallows but was prevented.'

The writer goes on to complain that the executioner was not sufficiently expert and produced ropes that were too short. Others had to be sent for which meant an hour's delay. 'Young Mills,' says the correspondent, 'amused himself most of the time in looking up at the executioner who sat across the gallows, and smiled several times as is supposed at the hangman''s going so awkwardly about his work. Tapner and Carter were very devout and gave a great deal of good advice to the spectators, the former recommended in a very strong manner to the Dragoons and soldiers who attended the execution to be very vigilant in their endeavours to take one Richards who he said was one of the worst of the gang and the principal cause of his coming to so shameful an end.'

'Major' Mills, defiant to the last, had to stand on tiptoe as the rope went round his neck. It was still too short. 'Don't hang me by inches,' he called out. Perhaps he remembered poor Chater's end.

And finally the horse was driven away and the six murderers were left to dance 'the hempen jig'.

Carter's body was placed on the gibbet at Rake; Chapman's at Rooks Hill near Chichester; Cobby's and Hammond's corpses were sited near Selsey Bill. The bodies of the two Mills, along with Jackson's, were flung into a hole near the gallows.

And the others? 'Little Harry' Sheerman was hanged after East Grinstead assizes some months later and he too was gibbeted at Rake. At the same assizes John Mills, son of 'Major', was found guilty of a brutal murder and hanged on Slindon Common. He was the third member of his family to be executed in three months. Edmond Richards, one of Galley's murderers, was hanged at Lewes in July 1749 and gibbeted on Hambrook common.

Thanks to the further testimony of Steel and Raiss, ten men, including Richard Perrin, William Farrell and Thomas Kingsmill, the leading lights in the Poole Customs House raid, and one woman, were sentenced to death in April 1749.

And it was this matter at Poole which had in the first place led to the horrific murders of two decent old men. Their murders resulted in such a wave of revulsion that not only were the murderers brought to book but the smuggling fraternity received a blow from which it never quite recovered. Though smuggling would continue in great volume, never again would smugglers threaten the rule of law in so brutal and scornful a manner.

Sally Churchman's Snuff

> A coward's weapon? Not so much. Poison is the weapon
> of the emotionless, the sociopath, the truly cruel.
> *Lady Killers: Deadly Women Throughout History*, Tori Telfer

Poor James Whale, a labourer in his thirties, just another young death in an age when such a short life was not remarkable. Horsham parish church burial register records his passing somewhat starkly: '1751 October 13, James Wale [*sic*], a poor man.' It does not record that he left a wife, only twenty years of age and a year-old child. How would they now manage? Would it be the workhouse? A life of meagre handouts from the parish overseers? After all, her husband had been, as the register stated, 'poor'. Oddly enough, neither of these prospects was likely, for when she reached twenty-one, Anne was due to inherit from an uncle the sum of £80 (approximately £18,300 today).

At first, Anne must be experiencing some serious anxieties, as well she might, for after all she has murdered her rather staid husband. But once 'a visitation of Almighty God' has been declared by the authorities, she doubtless feels a load lifted. Perhaps she intends returning to her former boisterous, carefree life. It will certainly be different now she's free of her deadly dull husband.

But how has it come to this pass? It's not as if life has ever been hard for Anne. She's the daughter of highly respectable parents, well-known in Horsham where her late father, William Waterton, had been a butcher. They had lived happily, the Watertons – there is no reason to think otherwise – at an inn on The Carfax.

But there had been warning signs. Anne was never an easy child and once her father died her mother was unable to keep her under control. So Anne grew into young womanhood showing less and less inclination to behave with any kind of moderation. For a while she left home, mixing with all kinds of dubious characters. Certainly not the kinds of people her parents had ever mixed with socially. But then Anne, quite uncharacteristically, suddenly decided at the age of eighteen to reform herself and settle down. It is not clear why she changed so but she seems to have made some resolution to mend her ways and return home to her mother.

What is astonishing is that in double-quick time, in 1749, the 18-year-old was married to James Whale. She seems to have put up no resistance to her mother's suggestion that, though he was only a labourer, he was the right man for her. He was sober and reliable, possessed of all those virtues a mother might see as desirable in a son-in-law. Within ten days of meeting James, Anne was married. Perhaps ten days is a rather brief time for a courtship but in this case her mother, perhaps desperate to find someone who would keep Anne from her past follies, urged the match. So, married, off they moved, the young couple, ending up in August 1750 at Corseletts on Broadbridge Heath, renting part of a farmhouse cottage where her cousin, Sarah Pledge, was already installed with her husband, another James, and their seven children.

From the start, it was an unholy alliance, this union of cousins. Older than Anne by several years, Sarah might have been expected to be rather more sober and mature, someone who might restrain a wilful younger cousin. But it is as if Ann deliberately sought out Sarah as someone as unreliable as herself. Perhaps had James Whale been aware of Sarah's real disposition, her hidden characteristics and inclinations, he might never have moved to Corseletts. He had nothing in common with either the coarse Sarah or her untrustworthy husband, James Pledge.

James Whales' stay at Corseletts was deeply unhappy. He fell out with the Pledges, at one time barring the crude and vulgar Sarah from his part of the house. He even tried to forbid Anne from talking to Sarah, convinced that she was a bad influence. There must have been so many embarrassing situations, living so close together in an atmosphere of such hostility.

And where Anne stood in all of this was obvious. She sided with her cousin, that devious and ill-natured woman, who encouraged the deepening rift between husband and wife. Whales' disapproval of his wife's relatives increasingly soured the marriage. Was James Whales fearful that under the influence of the Pledges his wife would squander her money? He was a worker, a saver, a man with an eye to the future. Not that he was to have much of a future.

Anne, of course, resented her husband's always wanting her to be prudent with her £80 inheritance. It was a very useful sum though not a princely fortune. By today's reckoning, it would be a very decent windfall but one which could be easily frittered away. James Whale knew of his wife's reckless ways with money, knew of her somewhat ill-disciplined past, fearing that the Pledges would encourage her to spend more than she ought. But was the sober James's regularly counselling his wife to be thrifty ever listened to? Did he possibly too frequently, to the point of boredom, warn Anne not to trust Sarah and her husband? If so, might not such unwelcome advice irritate the young wife, make her wish she had never been married to such a dull dog, yearn more and more for the freedom that she now regretted having lost? This difficult situation continued over the months, the two women closer than ever, constantly in each other's company and increasingly impatient with Whale.

Around harvest time of 1751 one of the women broached the solution. Was it Anne? Or Sarah? Impossible to say, but out of their daily frustrations with James Whale they were gradually able to hint to each other how things might be resolved. Perhaps for some weeks they had skirted around the possibilities, not wishing to come out with the awful proposal, not daring to voice outright what they had been working towards over several months.

In her confession months later, Anne was to describe it as Sarah's bold proposal. At last she had come to the point. The unutterable had been uttered. 'I say let us get rid of this devil,' Sarah had said. And Anne was in bed at the time, nursing her newly born child. Didn't she recoil in horror, didn't she disown her cousin? Of course not.

'How?' was her response. She was all for ridding herself of her husband. And Sarah had already thought this out, knew what could be done and how. 'With poison,' she said.

Desperate measures are now needed if they are to carry out what they've both been thinking about for weeks, perhaps months, and Sarah has suddenly remembered an old folk poison. It is not a very complicated nor time-consuming task to catch a few spiders. Sarah tells Anne she is going to pour beer over the spiders and then she'll bake them. After they are baked and are hard and dry and black, she will take them between her finger and thumb and squeeze them to a powder. Then she'll put it into a bottle of beer. And when 'the Prince', as she calls James in her sneering way, has his supper and drinks the beer, 'all will be over and it will look like a normal death. Nobody will ever suspect'.

And now here's Sarah, handing over the bottle to Anne. It's ready for James to sup with his evening meal. But next day James is alive and as well as ever. It seems the potion has had no effect. Anne's courage has failed her and she has thrown away the contents of the bottle in a ditch. But why? Has she changed her mind? Is she backing out? Is she worried that she will be the only one blamed should things go awry?

In any event, when Sarah comes back to see her that evening, hoping for news, hoping that James is already dead, she finds him hale and hearty. 'What has happened?' Sarah asks. Anne dares not tell her how she has disposed of the beer. All she says is that it hasn't worked. 'He hasn't even been sick,' she tells Sarah.

But Sarah isn't to be beaten. Off she goes to several villages, full of enthusiasm for the task. But on two or three occasions, once through an apothecary's door, her nerve fails her. She has doubts. Will whoever serves her remember her? Supposing their plan goes wrong. She falters more than once. But finally she goes to Horsham. It's a small place – only two thousand inhabitants where everybody knows everybody else. But her courage fails her yet again and she returns home without a purchase.

On Sarah's return, perhaps frustrated at the progress of the plan, Anne asks if Sarah's husband knows anything about poisoning. 'Go and talk to him yourself,' Sarah tells her and Anne, her hopes high once more, seeks him out.

'What shall I do to get rid of my miserable man?' Anne asks James Pledge.

'I'll tell you how,' James answers, seemingly unsurprised. And you begin to wonder about him. Is he already aware of the plotting? How deeply is he involved in it? Has he been stirring the pot for the last few months?

'Get a pennyworth of arsenic,' he tells Anne. 'It's very much like loaf sugar. Put it into some tea or some beer, sweeten it well and he won't taste it for it has no taste at all. It is only a little brackish.'

Arsenic is so easy to come by. At that time, any little village shop would sell you arsenic, that king of poisons. You'd just tell them you had mice or rats and no questions were asked. You didn't have to sign any forms or anything of that nature.

'And if I do it, how shall I be able to keep my child and pay such a large rent?' Anne, the girl with the comfortable inheritance, asks Sarah, who says that she can live with them rent-free as long as she is a widow, which further convinces Anne that she should proceed in her purpose.

Sarah goes off once more, more confident now as a result of what her husband has advised Anne what must be done.

And she's in Horsham once again. There has been too much talk, too much shilly-shallying. This time she buys a pennyworth of arsenic. It is not all that difficult. She has rats, she tells the apothecary, Mr Harfoy. She needs to get rid of them. And it's as easy as that.

At breakfast time the following morning, Sarah goes in to see Anne. She hands her the packet of poison. When Anne looks at it, she says, she can't believe the powder to be poison. 'Surely it's salts,' she says to Sarah, who replies somewhat sharply.

'By God, it is poison,' she says, 'and it is that which shall do for your husband.' After all the trouble she's gone to, here's Anne doubting her. 'And you want to do it, don't you?' Sarah asks her.

Anne is hesitant now, dubious about what they are up to, unable to do the deed when it comes to the pinch. 'If we do it, we shall all be took up and hanged,' she says but Sarah urges her on, reassures her, urges her be reasonable.

'No, it will never be found out if you don't tell but, by God, you shall have a hand in it or else you will tell.' Sarah is the dominant figure in this matter, keeping her cousin in the right frame of mind. But she's thinking that she needs some kind of reassurance. Sarah is not going to do it by herself.

'But there is really nothing to fear,' she tells Anne. She says she's done something like this before and has got away with it.

Has she? Really?

Sarah is so keen and it's difficult to assess the reason for her enthusiasm. Can it really be a promise of money? Or is it something more dreadful, a simple desire to murder? She goes on reassuring Anne that she knows how the poison has to be administered. She'll have to make a hasty pudding for James's dinner the next day.

The next day, Wednesday, 9 October, James has come home from work and perhaps he is looking forward to the hasty pudding, one of his favourites. He cuddles the baby while the meal is prepared. Sarah just pops in by chance, as it were – James has not succeeded in putting a permanent stop to the women talking together – and she hands Anne a paper bag. 'Here's the snuff Sally Churchman's sent to you,' Sarah says. Does she wink? Does she smirk? Anne, playing her part, thanks her and Sarah leaves for home.

Anne busies herself mixing the flour and milk, butter and sugar and eggs for the hasty pudding. It is a quick enough dish to make, as its name suggests. Soon it is ready and Anne upturns the pot in which it has been cooked and out it comes. James had been too busy with the baby to see her sprinkle the powder into the pan. When it comes to serving, she takes the top part of the pudding. She might even have given a tiny spoonful to the baby but the greater portion of it is for her husband who has been hard at work all day. He sets about that pudding and presumably enjoys it, scraping away every last morsel.

In the course of the evening James is sick, though not ill enough to prevent his going across to see Mr Agate, his landlord. He has paid his rent already and, responsible man that he is, has gone to seek a receipt. He experiences no ill effects from his meal. There are none of the problems that might have been expected. On the way back, however, and just as he reaches home, he has to lean over the fence, violently sick. He staggers into the house and goes straight upstairs to bed. Anne presumably attends to him, expresses concern but finds time to visit the Pledges, ostensibly to borrow a warming pan but principally to report progress.

The following day James continues very ill and Anne has to call on two male neighbours to help her lift him back into bed. He has been seriously ill all night and is on the point of death. He must have eaten a considerable quantity of arsenic for it to have had such an immediate and drastic effect upon him.

By eight o'clock that evening James Whale is dead. But straightaway the neighbours are suspicious. Why? Have the women's intentions been so blatant? For whatever reason, the neighbours call for a surgeon's opinion. There follows an inquest by coroner's jury who attribute James Whale's sudden death to 'a visitation by Almighty God'. What a relief. From now everything must have seemed right for the two women. The weeks pass and James Whale's death takes a back shelf.

It's months later, late spring, when Mr Agate, the Whales' landlord, has occasion to visit Mr Harfoy, the Horsham apothecary. In the course of a brief over-the-counter conversation, Harfoy, just chatting, happens to ask Agate about the rats.

The rats? What rats? Has Mr Agate heard him aright? What does Mr Harfoy mean by his remark? Oh, the rats that they'd been having trouble with last year, the ones that Mrs Pledge came about, the ones she bought a pennyworth of poison for. The query bemuses Mr Agate. Perhaps he's forgotten all about it. Possibly Mrs Pledge had taken it upon herself to try to cure the problem. Perhaps she hadn't wished to bother him with such a petty matter. Common enough, rats. Most people dealt with those sorts of things themselves. Nothing much to get excited about.

Or perhaps . . . and then, come to think of it . . . and the more Mr Agate thinks about his conversation with the apothecary, the more concerned he becomes. After all, James Whale's end was so sudden, so unexpected. Had his death been occasioned by some sinister arts? It's all worrying enough for Agate to seek advice from a magistrate. Whether there was a second exhumation is not known, though it is unlikely. After all, no doctor had knowledge enough to analyse victims' organs to prove the use of poison.

But certainly there's some unease among the magistracy and it all leads to Anne Whale and Sarah Pledge being taken into custody. They have to appear before a magistrate. At length both women, overawed perhaps by their situation, present an account of the murder which they sign. They do not personally admit murder. It's a case of each one laying the blame on the other, each pointing a finger at her cousin. Both versions endeavour to minimise the author's responsibility. Well, it will be resolved soon. Anne and Sarah, each determined that her accomplice will be held responsible, are committed to Horsham gaol. Remarkably, on the face of it, James Pledge appeared as guilty as the two women, but he was discharged prior to the trial at Horsham Assizes on 20 July 1752.

Anne and Sarah had effectively condemned each other in their original statements and they repeated their sides of the story before a judge and jury. Just as Anne cast much of the blame on her cousin, so did Sarah blame Anne. Sarah told how Anne had approached her about getting rid of her husband. Apparently Anne had promised Sarah that if she would buy a pennyworth of poison, she would give her a half-guinea to buy a new gown. In addition, Anne had apparently said that if she was caught and hanged she would leave Sarah £10 to look after her child.

The jury reached its inevitable conclusion. Guilty, both women. Their punishments were not to be identical. In the case of Sarah Pledge, the judge pronounced 'Let her be hanged by the neck and her body be dissected on Friday, 24 July.'

For Anne Whale was reserved the old punishment for petty treason. Blackstone's Commentaries on the Laws of England (1765–1769) describe petty treason as happening in three ways: by a servant killing his master; by a wife killing her husband; or by an ecclesiastical person killing his superior. Husbands, masters and superior churchmen are owed faith and obedience. And the pronouncement of the punishment of Anne for this gross betrayal reads thus: 'Let her be taken from the jail and thence to be drawn upon a hurdle to the place of execution and there to be burned with fire on Friday 24 July.'

And so it came to pass. For some time after conviction, Sarah Pledge behaved violently, swearing vehemently and threatening to fight the hangman at the place of execution. For her part, Anne Whale, the young mother, acknowledged the justice of the sentence and showed signs being penitent.

The executions took place on Broadbridge Heath in front of a huge crowd. Sarah, as was custom, was taken by cart. At 3:30 she was hanged, and her screams as she stood under the rope, so it was said, could be heard two miles away.

Two hours later Anne was chained to the stake. She prayed with the priest for upwards of half an hour. Then a huge fire was kindled, likely to burn for twenty-four hours, in front of one of the greatest crowds ever at this execution site. Before the flames reached her, the executioner strangled her. It all seems to have been highly satisfactory, one newspaper declaring it to have been carried out 'with the strictest decorum and decency'.

After hanging, the body of Sarah Pledge was put into a tallow chandler's hamper and, in accordance with the murder Act of 1752, it was taken to a barber-surgeon in Torrington for dissection. This gruesome post-mortem punishment was a common carefully choreographed public spectacle and as important, if not more, than the execution itself. It gathered a significant crowd.

Ah, the good old days.

Mass Murder on the High Seas

James Walvin, author of *The Zong*, describes this
as a case of 'mass murder masquerading as an insurance claim'.

The stink of it. You wouldn't believe it. Vomit, sweat, shit and, worst of all, the stink of fear about their future. That is, if there was a future for these poor, beleaguered folk, these men, women and children down there in the darkness of the hold where so many of them lay manacled, chained in pairs by wrist and ankle with scarcely room to move. From time to time they were let loose up on deck in limited numbers but most of them just lay there, down all their days, in their constricted spaces, amid the lurching of the boat and the creaking of its timbers and the endless groans, weeping and wailing. It must have seemed to the 420 poor wretches that they had been lying there for ever. And you can't be surprised that so many died of the various contagions that they had brought aboard.

The Zong had been captured only recently during the renewal of the war with the Dutch after a hundred years' lapse. The Dutch had used this vessel for slave trading for the past several years. In March 1781 the captured boat had been bought by a syndicate of wealthy merchants headed by William Gregson, up in Liverpool. It ought to be remarked that Gregson, like twenty-four other powerful slave traders in the city, was Lord Mayor of Liverpool as later his son was to be. It was a time when the trade was being increasingly questioned. The responses, such as the following in 1787, indicates the attitude of the slave traders to those calling out for abolition: 'The trade had been legally and uninterruptedly carried on for centuries past by many of His Majesty's subjects, with advantages to the country, both important and extensive but had lately been unjustly reprobated as impolitic and inhuman.'

Of course, like all property, it was insured with another company, also in Liverpool. The ship and its human contents were underwritten to the tune of £8,000 – big money, in today's terms possibly £1,500,000. So these black prisoners were valuable cargo and the more of them you could cram aboard, the more profit to swell the bank accounts of the white fellers in Liverpool.

Inevitably, there were deaths, what is described as 'wastage' but that's only to be expected. Of course, the men and women in their 'quarters' –

rather a grand word to use for folk in that situation – had rarely been too well cared for by the Arab traders who'd captured them in the first place. And anyway, wherever you were in Africa, you were prone to every manner of disease with only home remedies or the juju man to restore you back to good health. Your potential slaves weren't always in the best of health.

So then, in August 1781, here's the Zong setting off from Ghana and crewed by only seventeen men and captained by the recently appointed Luke Collingwood. They are bound for Jamaica with over four hundred poor souls cramped down in the hold. The Zong was intended to carry only half that number, but space is money.

Luke Collingwood's captaincy is a puzzle. Maybe he had influence. Perhaps he had a financial stake in the arrangements. He'd served on ships for some years though not as skipper. In fact he had precisely the wrong qualifications and experience for such a task. Up to now, he'd been working on ships as a doctor. Now that was an advantage one might have thought, given that his cargo had to be kept fit. Wasn't he the boy to ensure that, especially as the health of the cargo became increasingly problematic? And worse still the boat was running short of drinking water. They would have taken on fresh water in Jamaica but somehow they had managed not to find it, managed in fact to sail right past it. Of course, Collingwood would have to take responsibility for that, but was there no experienced navigator on board? Seems not.

So what are they to do when they realise they are so far away from Jamaica, three hundred miles away? And the crew, they turn to the captain, that former medical man, that man who like all in his great profession, had taken the Hippocratic oath. And the first element of that significant professional declaration is 'First do no harm'. Collingwood, however, interprets this wrongly. He is determined to do no harm to the ship owners' profits. And what follows is his beyond wicked decision to sacrifice some of his cargo.

He will claim that the ship had run short of water and matters were desperate. Overcrowding, malnutrition, accidents and disease had already killed seven of the crew as well as approximately sixty-two of the Africans but it was to get much worse. And think on this: ships' surgeons in Africa were typically involved in the selection and purchase of kidnapped people. They assessed the physical fitness of captives. Would they be salesworthy at their destinations? And supposing the surgeon rejected a captive, indicating that he was of no or little value, the Arab traders who had brought him would have no compunction about killing him. It is not unlikely that Collingwood had already witnessed the killing of 'rejects'. Did such experiences harden him to the degree that the code of medical ethics no longer had meaning for him? Does that help to explain the massacre on the Zong.

This is a grave situation and Captain Collingwood summons the crew together. Are they there to discuss the ethics of what the skipper suggests? Are they horrified at the very thought of the plan? Bear in mind that several crew members have already died. Anyway, they listen to Collingwood's suggestion and it is supported unanimously. Did some have feelings which they did not express, or did they think if they did not follow Captain Collingwood's suggestion they might also perish?

So, having reached a unanimous agreement to the captain's plan on 29 November, they set to work at once. On that day, fifty-four women and children were thrown through the cabin windows into the sea. How could the crew members responsible for gathering them up, by their armpits and their ankles, bear to do such a deed? Clearly they were not touched by conscience though they might have consoled themselves with the thought

that at least women and children brought financially less than adult men on the slave market. And in any case, did it matter? They were only blacks after all.

On the following day there was no attempt at a repeat of the deed. Perhaps it took that long to absorb the fact that they had murdered so many helpless souls. Perhaps the consolation was that at least white people weren't being thrown into the ocean. Perhaps they cast out of their minds the screams, the weeping, the feeble struggles, the babies' wretched whimpers. Only blacks, they'd tell themselves over and over. Only blacks going over the side.

Then, after a day's reflection, the crew turn to the male captives. On 1 December, forty-two men are bundled overboard. There were struggles, without doubt, though their victims were weakened by malnutrition and lack of exercise. But how do you imagine the strugglers were dealt with? Some of them were undoubtedly big strong fellers and fighting for their lives. So how were they dealt with? The imagination may provide answers.

And this disposal of their fellow human beings (yes, such a description of the blacks as human beings was unlikely to be accepted by some of their murderers) continued over the next few days. Principally it was those who were ill who were selected, but also perhaps those considered as nuisances were got rid of too. A final ten chose to commit suicide by jumping into the sea without any help. One of the captives suggested that the survivors, rather being thrown into the sea, should be denied all food and drink. Suggestion denied.

By the time the Zong reached Jamaica there were questions. Where were all the four hundred-odd cargo? There were 142 missing. What had happened? What is clear is that the questions were about missing numbers and the cost of the loss. No voices of sympathy or outrage are recorded.

Well, it was said, the blacks were thrown overboard because the ship did not have enough water to keep them alive. There were just too many of them wanting water and food. They couldn't keep up with such demands. So, they were asked, if that was the case how was it that there were 420 imperial gallons of water left when the Zong finally arrived in Jamaica on 22 December. One witness provided an answer to that query. It had rained heavily later on the voyage and some of the water barrels had filled up.

This was a great murder case. A mass murder case. An outrage against society, against humanity.

But no murder charges were ever brought. The ship owners had taken out insurance for their cargo of enslaved people and when the news of the disaster came they put in a compensation claim. When the insurers refused to cough up, the ship owners took them to court.

It was a commercial case which came before the courts where the ship's owners explained that the journey to Jamaica had, as a consequence of navigation errors, taken longer than expected.

The only solution arrived at was that which had been carried out. Extremely sad, of course, with the profits suffering, but that's business.

Then countering the claim of shortage of water came the information that the crew threw so many live slaves overboard. The truth of what happened was disputed, as is the considerable quantity of water with which the Zong arrived in Jamaica. And Collingwood had died before the case came to court.

Attempts were made to bring criminal charges against the late captain, the crew and the owners, but they were unsuccessful. The solicitor general, Justice John Lee, refused to take up the criminal charges.

'What is this claim that human people have been thrown overboard?' he asked. 'This is a case of chattels or goods. Blacks are goods and property; it is madness to accuse these well-serving honourable men of murder... The case is the same as if wood had been thrown overboard.'

On the same occasion, Lord Mansfield, judging the matter, declared that 'the Case of Slaves was the same as if Horses had been thrown overboard'.

Even the highest in the land were blind to kindness, fairness, justice . . . decency.

John Holloway, Owen Haggerty
and many others

Many that live deserve death. And some that die deserve life.
JRR Tolkien

It was worse than hell in the hulks, jam-packed with prisoners awaiting transportation to Australia or Jamaica. Under close supervision, often below decks and well battened down, at nights manacled, throughout the day flogged for the slightest infraction, this was a most demoralising and unhealthy environment for the several hundred convicts imprisoned below decks. Small wonder they took ill in great numbers. Illnesses such as cholera, dysentery and typhus were rife and convict mortality rates were high. And it was often months before the occupants were transferred to the vessels taking them to their far-off destinations.

It so happened that in late 1806 one of those destined for transportation, Benjamin Hanfield, already aboard, was ill enough to cause serious concern. Those in charge of such a cargo were well aware of the cunning tricks that might be played on them by the inmates for who would want to go the other end of the world and possibly never see friends and family again? But Hanfield, stuck here in Portsmouth and bound eventually for New South Wales, was weak and feverish and calling out for someone to listen to his story about a murder that had been committed four years earlier and he had been a witness. In fact, he was one of three men who had waylaid and murdered Mr John Cole Steele, the owner of the Lavender Warehouse in the Strand. Steele, a 35-year-old, had been visiting his nursery in Feltham and was on his way home when he was attacked.

No one had ever been taken up and charged with this murder but now, fearing that he was not long for this world, Hanfield begged the magistrates to listen to what he had to say. He had no wish to go to his grave with the memory of the murder of a decent man on that dark road on Hounslow Heath. And so a magistrate was summoned to hear what Hanfield had to say. But prior to meeting him, there must have been questions. Was this criminal really seriously ill or was it all a typically cunning attempt to gain a last-minute revision of his sentence? Was Hanfield genuinely conscience stricken? Or was he offering two men's lives and the resolution of an unsolved murder to save himself from transportation?

So a magistrate turned up and met Hanfield and the result was that the magistrate heard what to him sounded like a genuine death-bed confession. As a consequence, Hanfield was taken ashore and cared for and nursed with real concern while his account was considered.

In essence, Hanfield's story, which he related as he recuperated, was that back in November 1802 he had been approached by a friend, John Holloway, with a proposition to rob a business man who, on Saturday nights, regularly walked across the Heath on his way home from his workplace. Holloway had learnt about this man's habit that he used on such occasions, that on Saturday nights he carried on his person a significant sum of money after his week's business. Did Hanfield fancy a spot of 'low Toby'? Holloway had wondered. 'Low Toby'? Why not? Just up Hanfield's street. It wouldn't be his first job as a footpad. It might be more dashing to come the old Dick Turpin 'High Toby' game but he didn't have a horse. It would always have to be 'a feet on the ground' job for him.

And there'd be a third man along with them. One of their pals, a feller named Owen Haggerty. Best to work with people you know.

And the victim, Mr Steele. That business he had in the Strand, the Lavender Warehouse, must be doing well. He must be warm if he could base his business in such a location. What he must pay in rates and rent alone must be enormous. Sums like that would keep ten families in comfort.

This was just the kind of case liked by those who maintain the law. An unsolved case from four years back. A case with a witness, a man who had been present. At least, a man who claimed to have been present, at the murder of a respectable man, attacked brutally by men already known to the authorities.

Holloway and Haggerty were found relatively easily. They were known figures, though neither had been previously questioned about murder. They weren't top bracket law-breakers. But just look at them. Look at how obvious a criminal Holloway was. The newspapers were later to describe him as 'about forty years of age, of great muscular strength, tall, and of savage, brutal and ferocious countenance, with large thick lips, depressed nose and high check-bones'. Must be guilty with the kind of 'physog'. Of his companion, Owen Haggerty, only a little feller aged twenty-four, there were few lines in the press, but his association with a brute like Holloway would be enough to send him down for good and always.

The two accused appeared before the magistrate, Joseph Moser, in early 1807 and were charged with the murder. These words from the *Newgate Chronicle* are very telling: 'There was a great body of evidence adduced, none of which tended materially to incriminate the prisoners, except that of Hanfield, the accomplice, who under the promise of pardon had turned King's Evidence.'

The trial which began at the Old Bailey on 20 February, 1807, bears out this assertion. Both accused denied having robbed and murdered John Steele. All there was for the prosecution was Hanfield's statement as it appeared in the *Newgate Chronicle*. There really appears to be nothing else of moment, nothing incriminating. But there was Hanfield, at death's door in Portsmouth, so it seemed, when he claimed to have 'seen the light'. He had no wish to die with a guilty conscience. His statement, some weeks later, follows:

'I have known Haggerty eight or nine years, and Holloway six or seven. We were accustomed to meet at the Black Horse and Turk's Head public houses in Dyot Street. I was in their company in the month of November, 1802. Holloway, just before the murder, called me out from the Turk's Head and asked me if I had any objection to be in a good thing. I replied I had not. He said it was a 'Low Toby', meaning it was a footpad robbery. I asked when and where. He said he would let me know. We parted and two days after we met again, and Saturday, 6 November, was appointed. I asked who was to go with us. He replied that Haggerty had agreed to make one.

'We all three met on the Saturday at the Black Horse, when Holloway said: "Our business is to 'sarve' [obsolete – 'serve'] a gentleman on Hounslow Heath, who, I understand, travels that road with property." We then drank for about three or four hours and about the middle of the day we set off for Hounslow. We stopped at the Bell public house and took some porter. We proceeded from thence upon the road towards Belfont and expressed our hope that we should get a good booty. We stopped near the eleventh milestone and secreted ourselves in a clump of trees. While there the moon got up and Holloway said we had come too soon.

'After loitering about a considerable time, Holloway said he heard a footstep and we proceeded towards Belfont. We presently saw a man coming towards us and, on approaching him, we ordered him to stop, which he immediately did. Holloway went round him and told him to deliver. He [Steele] said we should have his money and hoped we would not ill-use him. The deceased put his hand in his pocket and gave Haggerty his money. I demanded his pocketbook. He replied that he had none. Holloway insisted that he had a book and if he did not deliver it he would knock him down. I then laid hold of his legs. Holloway stood at his head and said if he cried out he would knock out his brains. The deceased again said he hoped we would not ill use him. Haggerty proceeded to search him, when the deceased made some resistance and struggled so much that we got across the road. He cried out severely and as a carriage was coming up. Holloway said: "Take care. I will silence the bugger," and immediately struck him several violent blows on the head and body. The deceased heaved a heavy groan and stretched himself out lifeless.

'I felt alarmed and said: "John, you have killed the man." Holloway replied that it was a lie for he was only stunned. I said I would stay no longer and immediately set off towards London, leaving Holloway and Haggerty with the body. I came to Hounslow and stopped at the end of the town for nearly an hour.

'Holloway and Haggerty then came up and said they had done the trick and, as a token, put the deceased's hat into my hand. The hat Holloway went down in was like a soldier's hat. I told Holloway it was a cruel piece of business, and that I was sorry I had had any hand in it. We all turned down a lane and returned to London. As we went along I asked Holloway if he had got the pocket book. He replied that it was no matter, for as I had refused to share the danger, I should not share the booty. We came to the Black Horse in Dyot Street, had half a pint of gin, and parted . . . The next day I observed Holloway had a hat upon his head which was too small for him. I asked him if it was the same he had got the preceding night. He said it was. We met again on the Monday when I told Holloway that he acted imprudently in wearing the hat, as it might lead to a discovery. He put the hat into my hand, and I observed the name of Steele in it. I repeated my fears. At night Holloway brought the hat in a handkerchief and we went to Westminster Bridge, filled the hat with stones, and having tied the lining over it, threw it into the Thames.'

Hanfield, asked in cross examination why he had decided to confess to what had occurred, explained that it was pure chance that led to this disclosure of information. In Newgate, prior to his transfer to the hulk in Portsmouth, he had been talking with other prisoners of particular robberies that had taken place and the Hounslow robbery and murder came up. He had inadvertently said that there were only three persons who knew about that transaction. That he knew something of the case made his fellow prisoners wonder if he was going to 'turn nose'. It was never his intention to do that but now he feared his fellow prisoners might turn on him and he was obliged to hold his tongue lest he should be attacked.

This account did for the two accused men. As for their accuser, The *Newgate Chronicle* asserts at the end of the trial that 'their conviction rested upon the evidence of a wretch as base as themselves who stated himself to have been their accomplice'.

Mr Justice Le Blanc summed up the evidence, sounding relatively sympathetic towards Hanfield but, seemingly uncertain, he cautioned the jury to receive some of the evidence with caution.

The jury retired for fifteen minutes before returning a verdict of guilty. Holloway and Haggerty were sentenced to die on the following Monday morning.

The condemned men rose that morning at five, after a restless night during which they called out their claims of innocence. They washed, shaved and at seven were brought still shackled to the press room. Here their irons were removed

On the scaffold Holloway informed the sheriff that he wanted to make a public statement. Hopes rose. Was it to be a full confession? Presumably there was some disappointment when he simply reiterated his innocence. 'I am quite innocent of this affair,' he said. 'I never was with Hanfield. Nor do I know the spot. I will kneel and swear it.' Kneeling down, he called for curses on his head if he were not innocent. 'By God, I am innocent.' Then, for the hangman, it was back to business. Halters were placed round the necks of both men.

And the final gross touch. Elizabeth Godfrey joined the two men on the scaffold. She was to hang for killing a man in Marylebone on, of all days, 25 December, 1806. She had stabbed him in the eye, a wound from which he died.

So then, in unison, all three were launched into eternity. This morning, whatever the truth of the case against Holloway and Haggerty, there is no doubt that innocence died. For just as the trio on the staging died, so in the following hour or so did perhaps forty others.

The crowd which had gathered to witness these executions was unparalleled. Apparently 40,000 gathered outside Newgate to watch three fellow beings suffer the most appalling ritualised death. But these watchers were themselves beginning to experience quite terrible anxieties. Even before the principal actors had appeared, members of the audience were already crying out, desperate to escape from the heaving crowd. Pushing and shouting and in some cases praying out loud did not help those who felt the heavy pressure of the surrounding bodies.

There was a steadily growing confusion accompanied by desperate calls, wailing, screams of despair as well as the weeping of children – yes, children brought to this ghastly performance as though it were some kind of pantomime. Several women found themselves hemmed in. They called for help but in vain as they gradually slipped down and down till they lay on the ground, unaided and trampled upon, their cries unheard or ignored. Everyone was hemmed in. Should they lose their footing nothing could prevent their being trampled. Husbands and wives, mothers and children, could not be reunited. Some were to be lost from their loved ones for ever. From all parts came forlorn shrieks for help but such appeals for the most part went unanswered. Among the most vulnerable – the aged, the females and the children – were scenes of total helplessness as the fallen were ignored by those desperate to save themselves.

The scenes of greatest distress were at Green Arbour Lane. The terrible event which occurred here happened quite by chance. Two piemen, busy as usual at such an event, were the centre of what began as a slight accident. One of their baskets, placed on top of a stool, was knocked over and the owner bent down to pick it up. Then, presumably in bending down, he knocked over another man. Once over in this teeming mass, such was the unintentional violence of the mob, there was little chance of standing up again. And others, with no control over their movements, staggered and fell, never more to rise again, such was the unconscious violence of the mob. A man named Harrington was knocked over. Sad enough. But worse was that he was holding his twelve-year-old son's hand. The youngster fell too and he in was turn trampled to death.

A woman who was so imprudent as to bring with her her still breast-feeding child was one of those who perished. A man nearby, in the very act of falling, forced the child into the arms of yet another man, requesting him to save its life. This fellow, finding it required all his exertion to preserve himself, threw the infant into the arms of yet another man who, finding it difficult to ensure his or the child's safety, rid himself of the babe in a similar way. Finally, the child was again gathered by a man, who contrived to struggle with it to a cart, under which he deposited the infant until the danger was over.

And there was fighting as one beleaguered soul struggled against another to remain standing upright. A large body of the crowd was engaged in one convulsive struggle for survival, fighting furiously with other desperate mortals. And down went the old, the women, the children, the disabled. Here a cart overloaded with spectators broke down and some of the persons who fell from it were trampled underfoot and never recovered.

But finally, though there never could be any sense of order in such a situation, the struggles ceased, though the plaintive calls of anguish continued through the cold, grey morning hours.

Then they came to cut down the three bodies and the gallows tree was removed. The marshals and constables cleared the area. There was talk of a hundred dead and twenty-seven corpses were taken to St Bartholomew's Hospital, forty-two to St Sepulchre's church, one to the Swan on Snow Hill, one to a public house opposite St Andrew's church. An apprentice's corpse was carried to his employer's home on a shutter. A mother was seen carrying away the body of her dead boy. There was a sailor killed by suffocation opposite Newgate. He had been carrying a small bag of bread and cheese and he had come some distance to behold the execution.

After the dead, the dying and the wounded were eventually carried away, there were cartloads of shoes, hats, petticoats and other articles of clothing. Until late in the afternoon most of the local houses had some person needing some kind of medical attention.

In St Bartholomew's Hospital the bodies of the dead were stripped and then arranged around the walls on the first floor, on the women's side; they were placed on the floor with sheets over them, and their clothes placed as pillows at their heads; their faces were uncovered. People, relatives and friends for the most part were admitted to see the shocking spectacle and they went up one side of the rail, and returned on the other. Until two o'clock, entrances to the hospital were beset with mothers weeping for their sons, wives for their husbands and sisters for their brothers, and various others for their relatives and friends.

The next two days a coroner's inquest sat in at St Bartholomew's and at the other places where the bodies were located. The verdict recorded was 'that the several persons came by their death from compression and suffocation'.

The 'several persons' came to thirty-one. Between fifty and one hundred were injured.

A day to remember?

Oh yes, there'd been a hanging as well. Two men and a woman.

The Ratcliffe Road Murders

Many of our readers can remember the state of London just after the murder of Marr and Williamson; the terror which was on every face; the careful barring of doors; the providing of blunderbusses and watchmen's rattles.

Thomas Babington Macauley

For George Olney it's an ordinary enough day. It's 8 December, 1811, and he's on night duty. and it's midnight, more or less, and every hour's simply a duplicate of the one before. Night duty, well, nights can be good and bad. When you're round Gun Alley or Dung Wharf or Hangman's Gains, you're never sure what's round the corner, places like that. Always something unexpected on the old Ratcliffe Highway and so often something unpleasant, but it's quiet tonight. Just a few drunks. Nothing special to deal with. But it will be special. Except it's going to be special in a particular way. In fact, it'll turn out it's nothing like any other day of George Olney's life. Starting now.

'What's goin' on here?' he's wondering. 'Why's she hangin' round here this time o' night? And bangin' on the door like that.'

He's not having it. And Olney, the watchman, calls out to her, asking the girl what she thinks she's up to.

'I'm Margaret Jewell,' she says, 'and I live here.'

'Yes,' she answers his next question, 'I work for Mr an' Mrs Marr.'

Mr Marr has just recently set himself up here in the linen trade and he's doing well. After all, he's only twenty-four and he's his own boss already. Shows he's ambitious, that he's got what they call get-up-and-go.

'So you work here, eh?' Olney asks, not yet sure. Funny old place is Wapping. You never know. They're artful round here.

'Yes,' Margaret says. 'I went out to get some oysters but they're all gone now. All locked up.'

Not surprising they're locked up. They're sold out by now. Cheap street food like oysters sells out very quickly of a Saturday night, pay night. It might be past midnight but the streets are still busy.

'Anyway you're locked out,' the watchman says. 'Must've all gone to bed.'

They've never locked her out before. Margaret tells him. She's knocked and rung the bell several times. Mr Marr was still up when she passed the window not long ago because after looking for oysters she'd gone to pay a baker's bill at the other end of the road.

'An' I heard footsteps inside, him comin' down the stairs but he didn't open the door. And little Timothy was crying.'

'Well, that's what babies do at three months,' Olney says with the air of a man who has experienced fatherhood.

'Yes,' Margaret says. 'Must've forgotten about me and locked up for the night. After all it's late.' It was about ten past twelve.

At this point, Mr Murray from next door comes on the scene. He was just having a bite to eat and he's heard the chatter outside and some bumping in next door's house.

'She can't get in,' Olney tells Murray.

'Can't get in?' he says, quite decisively because he's a business man, a pawnbroker, in fact. 'I'll nip round the back,' he tells them. 'Maybe the back door's open.'

So round the back Murray goes and over the wall and into Marr's rear quarters. The back door's open and there's candlelight inside. He goes up the back steps and he's calling out to them that they haven't fastened their shutters at the front. Funny that, because young Marr is very careful as a rule. He's a very alert young feller.

Murray gives another shout. No reply. They're at home, he's sure of that. So now, not getting any response, he goes down the steps and into the back door to the shop. Odd, isn't it?

And he'll never forget it.

For the rest of his life what he sees here will stay with him.

There's a body lying on the floor. It's the lad, the apprentice, young James Gowan. And he's not moving. And his head, his face, is all smashed in. He's almost unrecognisable.

Blood and brain are splashed on the floor and on the walls. Even on the ceiling there are splashes of human matter. And there's a streamlet of blood, leading to the front door. As if perhaps he had gone there to the door to answer it. And had met his murderer.

Murray wonders what next to do because there's no sound in the house. Despite this room being bathed in horror, he decides to let Olney in the front door, but as he crosses the room, before he reaches the door, he stumbles.

Over a body. It's Celia, Marr's wife. Just a young woman, a young mother. Her skull battered, her blood still trickling across the floorboards.

Murray lets Olney in, warning the watchman that he's going to see a terrifying sight. And together, cautiously, for the perpetrator of these foul deeds might be lurking somewhere further inside the shadowy house, they edge their way. And then they find the owner, Timothy Marr, the third person to have been fiercely bludgeoned to death in this house tonight. He's behind the counter.

Good God, will it never end, this nightmare? No, it will not. Not for these two men. For these two it's never likely to be forgotten. For then, upstairs, they find the baby. Timothy, twelve weeks old. He's in his cradle. One side of the head is crushed. And worse, his throat has been cut so savagely that the head is all but severed.

Already there's a crowd gathering outside, for Wapping has no closing time. There are always people on the streets, night and day, for all sorts of dubious reasons. And soon on the scene, for they are so close to the river, along come a couple of members of the Thames River Police who somebody has sent for. One is Waterman Constable Charles Horton, the senior officer and most energetic investigator of the Marine Police Force based in Wapping High Street. Horton, businesslike, professional – rare qualities in upholders of the law at that time – he looks round, upstairs and down, checks the till in the shop. Still money in there. In one bedroom drawer he finds £152. Does he wonder how a twenty-four-year old man has accumulated such a sum? Why has it not been banked? This is Wapping, a dangerous area. This is dockland, at times a desperate kind of location. Why is the money left in such an unguarded place? Young Marr seems a fairly shrewd young feller if he can set up a business as he has done. But in the few months he has been here how can he have accumulated such an impressive sum of money? But these are questions which perhaps were never asked and certainly never answered.

But the questions do nag. Right to this day. These monstrous interlopers – and surely one man cannot have caused such havoc – why didn't they take anything? Or were they just there for the kill?

Maybe they ran off at the sound of Murray and Olney coming in the house. Was it then that they decided to silence the witnesses? Silence a baby? Had they been so desperate to escape from the house, would they have had time for such brutal attacks? If anxious to escape, would they have bothered to slaughter a baby so? Were these gross beatings, these murders, the principal objective of the intruders? Does this charnel house hint at anger, hatred, something personal?

Horton was of the view that the weapon used had been a ripping chisel. There was one found in the shop, but it was clean. Then in the bedroom, he found, leaning against a chair, a heavy shipwright's maul, a long-handled hammer, covered with blood, still wet. The murder weapon? On the heavy end were blood and hairs. At the other end, used for hammering in nails, the metal was chipped.

Outside, at the rear of the premises, there were two sets of footprints, each of which bore traces of blood as well as sawdust from carpentry work inside the house earlier in the day. These fresh tracks were followed into Pennington Street which ran behind the house and one witness said that shortly after the alarm was raised he'd seen ten or so men running away from a nearby empty house in the direction of New Gravel Lane. So was this the work of a gang? A question never answered.

On returning to his station Horton found three sailors already in custody. They'd been seen in the area earlier but none of them appeared to have anything to do with the atrocity. But it was enough that they were Portuguese. Foreigners on such occasions were always suspect. Later, but only after being greatly harassed, they were all released.

At least it was possible to work out the time of this obscene slaughter. It was committed between 11.55 pm when Margaret Jewell went out on her errands and 12.20am when she returned. John Murray, who had been so active in those early hours, had heard bumping noises at about 12.10am just before he left his house to investigate.

Cornelius Hart, a carpenter, who had worked in the shop that day, was detained and questioned but no case was made against him and he was released. Marr's brother also came under scrutiny as it was rumoured that there was a long-lasting rift between the two men. He was interrogated for 48 hours but he offered an alibi which was finally accepted.

Then there was a former girl servant at the house who had been dismissed months earlier when it was said that she had uttered death threats against Mrs Marr. She was questioned but it was clear she had nothing to do with the affair.

And so enquiries went on. Unsuccessfully. How could it have been otherwise? At this time there was no coherently organised body to pursue crime matters. The local constables were respectable but inexperienced, appointed for one year, and generally reluctant to investigate matters beyond their competence as this happening surely was. And anyway, who would wish to interfere too much in his neighbour's affairs? And what experience did the local magistrates have in dealing with so many cases? Generally, for the vast majority of those in authority, crime and crime-fighting, the law and its mysteries, were a massive complexity totally beyond their areas of competence.

Thank goodness they could call on the Bow Street people and the Thames river policemen. At least they brought some know-how to their work. Several of the Thames men worked with others investigating the crimes. Some of these men patrolled the streets of Wapping which served to reassure residents in this peculiarly frightening time. But for twelve long days nothing promising turned up.

But something did happen eventually, though it was far from promising. Another set of grotesque murders occurred at the King's Arms in New Gravel Lane, only a few minutes' walk from the scene of the first outrage. That evening a crowd, increasing by the minute, gathered outside the pub, astonished to see a nearly naked man climbing down from the second-floor window using knotted sheets. He was terribly upset, this fellow, almost hysterical. It was John Turner who, for the past eight months, had been one of John Williamson's lodgers. Terrified, he was calling out, 'Murder!'

Afterwards, under questioning, Turner said that he had gone to bed at about eleven o'clock. Then sometime later he'd heard Mrs Williamson call out 'Murder!' and then Bridget Harrington was shouting, 'We shall all be murdered!' After this, he heard John Williamson's despairing cry, 'I am a dead man!'

These desperate appeals did not conjure up any immediate desire on Turner's part to intervene and, indeed, at the very thought of the murderers in the house, his courage failed him. Others would think it outrageous that he later made his escape leaving the Williamsons' granddaughter undefended. But on such occasions, perhaps understandably, fear overcomes courage.

Turner, having heard the voices below, eventually steeled himself and left his bed to investigate. crept downstairs atip-toe and saw one of the intruders cutting Mrs Williamson's throat as well as rifling her pockets. He went back to his room. He had seen enough, though he did glimpse a second man. He took the sheets from his bed and fastened them together, lashing them to the bed posts. Then, climbing out of the window, gripping the sheets, he called down to the watchman below to sound the alarm. Then the watchman caught hold of him. Nearly naked. But he had escaped.

The crowd, brave in numbers, now forced open the doors and swarmed into the taproom. And there was the body of the landlord, John Williamson, face up. He had been beaten, had had his throat cut. His right leg was fractured. By his side was an iron crowbar. In trying to defend himself, his hand had been nearly severed at the wrist

In the parlour, were his wife Elizabeth and the maid Bridget. The faces of both women had been severely battered, their necks broken and their throats cut. Elizabeth's neck was severed deep into the bone. Bridget's feet were by the fire grate, suggesting that she had been about to lay the next morning's fire when she was attacked.

Searching upstairs the already excited searchers came across the 14-year-old granddaughter of the Williamsons. She was still in bed, still asleep. Mercifully she had heard nothing. She was hastily removed from the premises and taken to lodge with a relative several miles away.

The bodies were placed on their beds. As in the case of the Marrs murders, there was all-day access to view the corpses. To us a curious custom, its intention was intended to allow a respectful acknowledgement of the dead. A custom, too, which catered to the sensation seekers. And regrettably, serving also as an opportunity for pickpockets and all manner of other seedy folk willing to take advantage of the bereaved and any other unsuspecting folk.

But for the river police and the Bow Street Runners there was plenty for them to seek out. There were witnesses aplenty, encouraged perhaps by the handsome rewards on offer. Men of all ages and sizes and appearance were reported as likely culprits and rounded up. But there was no known link between the two murdered families and there seems to have been no obvious motive for either murder. Williamson's watch was missing. Had what had begun as a common burglary just gone wrong? It just doesn't seem feasible.

Apparently there'd been a tall man hanging about outside The King's Arms that night, a fellow wearing a long loose-fitting coat. In fact, earlier in the evening, a concerned John Williamson had spoken to the constable about this suspicious character. So now, off went several Bow Street Runners to hunt him down and they produced several men who might meet that description but who were released.

There were questions about John Turner, too, now recovering from his brief adventure. He had shouted for help. Had this scared the killer away? Unfortunately, no-one seemed sure about Turner and he was even regarded by some as a suspect. He underwent a rigorous questioning, principally because he had been a regular customer at the King's Arms, but eventually the poor man was exonerated.

Then some days later a new suspect came on the scene. John Williams. On the Thursday night when the crime was committed, Williams had not shown up at his lodgings at the nearby Pear Tree until around midnight. Granted, he was known to stay out late, enjoying himself, but given the circumstances his behaviour was now considered suspicious, especially since he had been seen near the Williamson home. Williams did not deny being at the King's Arms on the night in question. It was a place he went to regularly and in fact he regarded the Williamsons as good friends. One witness recalled how earlier on that dreadful night she had seen Mrs Williamson pat Williams on the face in a kindly, motherly way. But against that, how could he reconcile the fact that earlier on the day of the murder he had no money and then, after the murders, he had some?

True, but he claimed that he had money put by as he had to visit a doctor. In fact, that's where he went when he left the tavern earlier on that Thursday evening. He'd gone first to consult a surgeon about an old injury and then to a lady practitioner who was likely to be cheaper. This information was never checked. Yes, he said, he did have money in his pockets, but this had come only after he'd pawned some items of clothing.

Despite insisting on his innocence, Williams was remanded to Coldbath Fields prison, where another suspect was also confined. Until this crime was solved, officials were taking no chances and no one was going anywhere. In fact, in the belief that Williams had not acted alone, they would round up yet a third suspect.

Then, on Christmas Eve, came the first real break in the case. It was now more than two weeks after the Marr murders and five days after the Williamsons had been bludgeoned and hacked to death. The police now searched the Pear Tree public house, acting on a tip from the landlord who happened at that time to be in gaol for debt. The publican had heard that the police had found a maul marked with the initials JP or IP. 'Check a trunk that's been left with us,' the pub owner suggested. 'Its owner's one of our regular lodgers, John Peterson. He's at sea, but he keeps a maul in his trunk.' The landlord had recalled the initials on the maul and admitted that he had used it himself for the odd job round the pub. That was a significant lead.

At an open forum of witnesses that day, John Turner was asked if he could identify John Williams as the man he had seen standing over Mrs. Williamson. He said that he could not. A woman who washed Williams's clothing was then asked if she had washed any bloody clothing. She said that about two weeks earlier she had noticed that one shirt was torn and another had blood on the collar. She just thought Williams had been in a fight – he was an aggressive sort of man, at times, though he often came off second best. As she had not washed for him since before the Williamson murder, she really had nothing to say on that matter.

Williams tried to give an account of his torn and bloodstained shirt, describing a recent scuffle, but the magistrates silenced him. Tomorrow was another day, he was told. Nevertheless, it seems that Williams went back to his cell in good heart, and according to witnesses, confident that on the morrow he would be released.

The facts against John Williams were that as a lodger at the Pear Tree he'd had the opportunity to take Petersen's maul from where the landlord had stored it; that he'd had money after the murder but not before; that he'd returned to his room just after the killer had fled the second crime scene; and that he'd allegedly had a bloody and torn shirt.

The courts in those days generally relied on logic and eyewitness testimony over forensic evidence, although they did attempt to identify the maul and to ascertain whether the shirt in question did indeed have bloodstains on it. If a narrative could be devised that fitted the facts and made sense, then more than likely a person could be found guilty. They had not the knowledge, indeed, the science, to help them.

But Williams apparently remained confident. However, he never got to trial. Three days after Christmas, on December 28, he had used a scarf to hang himself from an iron bar in his cell at the Coldbath Fields. No one discovered his body until just before he was scheduled to go to court for a hearing. The court waited for Williams but all that happened was that an officer came to announce the dreadful news. The officials and public had gathered to hear more testimony and to ask Williams more questions but a lone police officer came simply to announce what had occurred. It was a surprise to many. He had been so optimistic of release. To some, however, it was almost an admission of guilt.

Many asked if it was a genuine act of suicide. Or was it even a murder sanctioned by the authorities? But one thing was clear. He wasn't going to get away with his awful crimes. And finally, the truth, as it appealed to the authorities, was that John Williams was guilty of the murders in both the

Marr and Williamson households. Others would say that John Williams was the eighth victim in this mysterious series of murders.

Assuming that Williams was connected with the murders in some way, and assuming that he did not act alone, who would be the prime suspects to benefit most from the authorities' unseemly haste to close the case as quickly as possible? Joint authors P.D. James and T.A. Critchley in their gripping book, *The Maul and The Pear Tree*, seem to think that Cornelius Hart, the carpenter working at the Marr's house, had a case to answer. His chisel, which had so mysteriously vanished prior to the murder of the Marrs, seems to have equally mysteriously reappeared in the shop on the morning after the murder. The obvious implication is that Hart brought it back to the shop with him, indicating that he was involved in whatever had occurred. Also, if Williams was damned by his being seen in the Kings Arms late on the night of December 19th, then his drinking partner, Ablass, must be every bit as suspect. In addition, Ablass bore a far more striking resemblance to the man seen standing over the body by Turner but Ablass, reputedly a violent man and who was detained for some time even after Williams's death, was finally released. Was this former shipmate of Williams and Marr a likely murderer? This possibility seems not to have been thoroughly explored.

Finally, what about Williams himself? Why should he choose to commit suicide before his second court appearance? The answers he had given at his initial interrogation had explained away most of the questions that he had been asked. Even if he were involved, he would surely have hoped to deflect suspicion away from himself a second time. Witnesses from the prison gave evidence that he did not seem at all concerned on the evening prior to his impending court appearance. Would he have even been aware of any fresh, albeit circumstantial evidence, which had been gathered against him? Also, given that he was manacled, how easy would it be for a man, secured in such a fashion, to hang himself across a beam in his cell?

We shall never know the truth, but could it be that Williams was in fact the eighth victim of the Ratcliffe Highway Murders? Was this a murder inside prison walls, a successful attempt to silence him lest he incriminated others? Whatever the case, in the opinion of many, his suicide was taken as an admission of guilt. To the authorities it mattered that somebody be caught if only to allay the public's anxieties.

But he's getting away with it. No trial. Not declared guilty. Won't do. The public – whoever they are – won't be satisfied with this. If they can't see him hanged at least let him be disgraced, reviled, put on show. And the home secretary, accepting the declaration of the Shadwell magistrates that Williams alone was responsible for both sets of murders, orders that his body be publicly paraded around the streets of Wapping and Shadwell.

And so on New Year's Eve 1811, John Williams is displayed to the ten thousand oddly silent people lining the streets. He lies on an open, horse-drawn cart along with the display of the maul, the chisel and the crowbar, the brutal instruments he is claimed to have used on his victims. He is driven where he is supposed to have roamed, with a ten-minute stop outside Marr's shop at 29 Ratcliffe Highway and later outside the Kings Arms. Finally the procession reaches the junction of Cable Street and Cannon Sreet Road, and here he will be buried.

The driver of the cart, of his own volition, whips Williams's face three times before the body is tumbled into the grave. Now the body is placed in a kneeling position and a stake is mallet-driven through his back towards where the heart is located. His body will lie in a grave so narrow, so short, so cramped, that he will be in eternal discomfort. Finally, earth is piled over the remains of John Williams. The whole barbarous process is completed.

John Williams, untried, not found guilty, murdered by the State.

Peterloo
16 August 1819

Rights are not gifts from one man to another, nor from one class of men to another. It is impossible to discover any origin of rights otherwise than in the origin of man; it consequently follows that rights appertain to man in right of his existence, and must therefore be equal to every man.

Thomas Paine

Today the sun has condescended to shine on Manchester and thousands have headed to St Peter's Field to listen to Henry Hunt, the great 'Orator Hunt', who'll expound his radical views, calling out, for example, for all males to have the vote and for the repeal of the Corn Laws which fall heavily on the pinched pockets of the poor. And he'll be up on the rostrum, in great form, and waving his white hat at the crowd. And below him, will be the ranks of those who have followed him in a great procession, their great colourful banners unfurled and carrying messages such as 'Universal Suffrage' and 'Unity and Strength'. Meanwhile the brass bands are still playing rousing tunes. There's something joyful about this day.

Here is Samuel Bamford, the radical thinker, recording the occasion: 'About half an hour after our arrival the sounds of music and reiterated shouts proclaimed the near approach of Mr Hunt and his party; and in a minute or two they were seen coming from Deansgate, preceded by a band of music and several flags. Their approach was hailed by one universal shout from probably 80,000 persons. They threaded their way slowly past us and through the crowd, which Hunt eyed, I thought, with almost as much of astonishment as satisfaction. This spectacle could not be otherwise in his view than solemnly impressive.'

And look how it has turned out. To stop such dangerous notions being broadcast, the Salford magistrates have summoned the mounted Manchester and Salford Yeomanry, of all people, to catch hold of Mr Hunt, up on the speaker's rostrum, and along they come in their smart blue jackets and white trousers and whooping as these bully-boys do when they're out a-hunting Mr Fox. These are not real soldiers, They are not soldierly. They are here with great smiles on their faces and laughter in their bellies, these men who delight in frightening non-combatants. All was going so well but then the mood changed.

Bamford writes: 'We had got to nearly the outside of the crowd, when a noise and strange murmur arose towards the church. Some persons said it was the Blackburn people coming, and I stood on tiptoe and looked in the direction whence the noise proceeded,and saw a party of cavalry in blue and white uniform come trotting, sword in hand, round the corner of a garden wall, and to the front of a row of new houses, where they reined up in a line. "The soldiers are here," I said; "we must go back and see what this means." "Oh," someone made reply, "they are only come to be ready if there should be any disturbance in the meeting."

' "Well, let us go back," I said, and we forced our way towards the colours. On the cavalry drawing up they were received with a shout of goodwill, as I understood it. They shouted again, waving their sabres over their heads; and then, slackening rein, and striking spur into their steeds, they dashed forward and began cutting the people . . . "Stand fast," I said, "they are riding upon us; stand fast."

'The cavalry were in confusion: they evidently could not, with all the weight of man and horse, penetrate that compact mass of human beings and their sabres were plied to hew a way through naked held-up hands and defenceless heads; and then chopped limbs and wound-gaping skulls were seen; and groans and cries were mingled with the din of that horrid confusion. Many females appeared as the crowd opened, and striplings or mere youths also were found. Their cries were piteous and heart-rending, and would, one might have supposed, have disarmed any human resentment: but here their appeals were in vain.'

These folk here today, they ought not to be ridden down, cursed at, punched, sabre-slashed or trodden under the hooves of the Yeomanrymen's mounts. But they are. And in their grand uniforms and mounted on the fine horses they've purchased out of their own pockets, on they go, these Yahoos, blundering through the tight-wedged masses of folk, these amateur cavalry men, these wealthy part-time warriors, so that they may reach Hunt more quickly and silence him before he poisons more minds with his liberal views. Run away, old woman, run away young miss, but it's not easy for you to do so in this melee. Nor is it easy for young lads and old men. This is sport dressed up as official control.

Bamford continues: 'In ten minutes from the commencement of the havoc the field was an open and almost deserted space. The sun looked down through a sultry and motionless air. The curtains and blinds of the windows within view were all closed. The hustings remained, with a few broken and hewed flag-staves erect, and a torn and gashed banner or two dropping; whilst over the whole field were strewed caps, bonnets, hats, shawls, and shoes, and other parts of male and female dress, trampled, torn, and bloody.

'Several mounds of human being still remained where they had fallen, crushed down and smothered. Some of these still groaning, others with staring eyes, were gasping for breath, and others would never breathe more.'

The first account of the atrocity was recorded by Haigh Allen, a young magistrate from Huddersfield, who was in Manchester to monitor events, barely an hour after the massacre. He seems not dissatisfied with the way in which things have turned out.

'Gents,' he wrote at 2.30pm. 'The meeting took place at 1 o'clock. Hunt in the chair with 16 flags and 7 caps of Liberty hoisted up amongst upwards of 60,000 people, the cavalry has just broke in upon them, the flags are taken, Hunt and his party secured, several lives are lost and a number wounded. The cavalry are now securing the streets in all directions, ½ past 2 o'clock, Yours H. Allen.'

Sixty thousand people. Four hundred and thirty casualties. Or perhaps more. All civilians out for the day, free from the factory and the mill and the fields they once had shared, and fourteen of them (fifteen if you count the unborn child of Elizabeth Gaunt who was beaten by a constable) now lie dead, young and old, men, women and children and an eighteen-year old lad who four years earlier had beaten his drum at Waterloo and who now lay as a victim on this occasion already dubbed with appropriate scorn, 'Peterloo'. What levelling politics had lured the boy there? None most likely. Like so many, he was having a day out.

On the following day printed notices and pamphlets appeared which clearly ignore what had occurred. It was the unruly masses who were culpable. The men. But what of the women? What of the children? Why no mention of them?

Peterloo. A day of shame.

The following lines come from Shelley's 91-verse poem, *The Masque of Anarchy*, written shortly after the outrage but not published until 1832. The editor, Leigh Hunt, withheld it from publication in *The Examiner* in 1819 because he 'thought that the public at large had not become sufficiently discerning to do justice to the sincerity and kind-heartedness of the spirit that walked in this flaming robe of verse.'

> As I lay asleep in Italy
> There came a voice from over the Sea
> And with great power it forth led me
> To walk in the visions of Poesy.
> I met Murder on the way –
> He had a mask like Castlereagh* –
> Very smooth he looked, yet grim;
> Seven blood-hounds followed him:
> All were fat; and well they might
> Be in admirable plight,
> For one by one, and two by two,
> He tossed the human hearts to chew
> Which from his wide cloak he drew.
> Next came Fraud, and he had on,
> Like Eldon,** an ermined gown;
> His big tears, for he wept well,
> Turned to mill-stones as they fell.

* *The Tory leader in the House of Commons.*
** *The lord chancellor.*

The Cato Street Conspiracy

Rulers who neither see, nor feel, nor know,
But leech-like to their fainting country cling
Till they drop, blind in blood, without a blow

So writes Shelley in his poem, *England*, in 1819. He has seen the future and warns of desperate times ahead unless there are changes. We've already had the mini-massacre at Peterloo; we've had Parliament's so-called 'Gag' Acts which have stifled our countrymen's freedoms, and years earlier a Swiss philosopher, Jean-Jacques Rousseau, had warned Europe that 'man is born free but is everywhere in chains'.

And now, on 23 February 1820, the Bow Street Runners have arrested eleven plotters from the upper floor of a barn in Cato Street, just off the Edgeware Road, right at the end of the city where in the near beyond there are pastures and woodlands and farms. This terrifying plot was intended to raise the masses throughout the land and they'd overthrow the government, set up a Committee of Public Safety intending to reshuffle the whole social and political order (an echo here of France when from 1793 to 1794 their similarly titled government ushered in the monstrous Reign of Terror). But here, in England, the principal plan was to make life better for ordinary people.

But only eleven men arrested from what is considered to be a nationwide conspiracy? Yes, and simply because the whole business is doomed from the outset.

The members of the Cabinet were not suddenly swooped upon on 23 February 1820 at a dinner at Lord Harrowby's home at 39 Grosvenor Square. Oh yes, that was the intention. One of the plotters would knock at the door, claiming to be delivering a parcel and when the door was opened, in they'd charge, a dozen or so, and they'd cause havoc with hand grenades and the Cabinet members would be slaughtered and two of the victims, the deeply reviled Lords Castlereagh and Sidmouth, would suffer the supreme indignity of having their heads cut off and put on public display on the spikes of Westminster Bridge. Such breathless stuff, sudden, unexpected and powerful. They'd also capture cannon from the artillery ground at Finsbury, take over the Bank of England and distribute its coinage, burning the paper currency as valueless. Land held by the aristocracy would in future be held in common.

The conspirators have deluded themselves that a grateful working class will rise in support of their provisional government. A real revolution, eh? But the plot fails. The Cato Street conspirators have been led into a trap by members of the government's extensive spy organisation. In reality, there is no grand dinner taking place that evening. None of the Cabinet members will be at Grosvenor Square. It's all a ruse and, would you believe it, the second in command of the conspirators, George Edwards, a seeming enthusiastic recruit to their ranks, one of the most vociferous at their meetings, one of those calling for the bloodiest action, is himself a spy and agent provocateur.

In his relatively brief time as a member of group, Edwards has impressed their leader Arthur Thistlewood who, despite the misgivings others had, in December 1819 appointed him as his aide-de-camp. Edwards has constantly urged more and more threatening deeds, with the ultimate plan to murder senior government ministers in Grosvenor Square. But throughout these weeks Edwards is sending a regular stream of written reports to John Stafford, chief clerk at Bow Street.

And so the men are captured even before they even leave Cato Street and now await trial. But they won't see George Edwards there. He will not be called as a witness, nor will he ever be mentioned in court. No one will question him about how he so forcefully called for the ruthless, blood-letting of Cabinet members, men who according to this agent provocateur, fully deserved to die. With a new identity, now naming him as George Parker, he's in Guernsey and shortly he'll be spirited away to South Africa.

But let me tell you a little more about Edwards, for his betraying the conspirators has little to do with conscience or belief or principle: rather it is about money, about elevating his position, bettering himself. When first he made himself known to the conspirators he was but modestly dressed, as if he hadn't two pennies to rub together. Why didn't somebody remark on the fact that as the weeks went by he was markedly better dressed? Where'd the money come from?

So, anyway, the Bow Street men arrive at the Cato Street address and clamber up the ladder to the loft where they surprise the would-be revolutionaries who are more or less on the point of setting off for a fifteen-minute walk to Grosvenor Square.

Such an uproar now. What's happening? The conspirators scramble for their weapons. Arthur Thistlewood, a former army officer, draws his sword and kills with one thrust Richard Simkins, one of the men coming up from the ladder. And then, quite unexpectedly, all lamps are doused, all candles snuffed and in the dark no-one dares to shoot and there's a scramble, a mad dash, a pushing and a pulling of men, Runners and conspirators alike, all making for the exit, all trying to get out of this darkness, to get downstairs. It appears that of the thirty or so plotters who were upstairs when the Runners and the soldiers arrived, perhaps twenty of them have escaped. Including Thistlewood, but he is picked up the following morning. Not at his own lodgings but at another place. Somebody, quite early on, aiming to save his own skin, has let the Runners know where Thistlewood is hiding out. And when they come to pick him up, here he is, Arthur Thistlewood, still a-bed at nine o'clock of the morning, still wearing his stockings and britches, while his military-style sash lies on a chair by the bed.

Once they've handcuffed him, Thistlewood is taken before a magistrate for these matters must be done formally, and after that it's off to Whitehall to appear before the Privy Council where he makes no response to their queries.

At the trial at the Old Bailey from Monday 17 April 1820 until the sentencing on Friday 28 April, the outcome was never in doubt. Five were sentenced to death: Thistlewood, Richard Tidd, James Ings, William Davidson and John Brunt. Five others: James Wilson, John Strange, Charles Cooper, John Harrison and Richard Bradburn were sentenced to transportation for life.

Thistlewood was calm throughout the trial, making a powerful final statement against a reactionary government. When he was asked the formal question by the clerk of arraigns, why he should not receive the death sentence, he read a lengthy commentary of which some sections are presented here:

'I applied to the court to hear my witnesses: the court inhumanly [*sic*] refused, and I am in consequence to be consigned to the scaffold . . . A few hours hence I shall be no more, but the nightly breeze which shall whistle over the silent grave that shall protect me from its keenness, will bear to your restless pillow the memory of one, who lived but for his country, and died when liberty and justice had been driven from its confines, by a set of villains, whose thirst for blood is only to be equalled by their activity in plunder . . .

'I am asked, my lord, what I have to say that judgment of death should not be passed upon me according to law. This to me is mockery – for were the reasons I could offer incontrovertible, and were they enforced even by the eloquence of a Cicero, still would the vengeance of my Lords Castlereagh and Sidmouth be satiated only in the purple stream which circulates through a heart more enthusiastically vibrating to every impulse of patriotism and honour, than that of any of those privileged traitors to their country, who lord it over the lives and property of the sovereign people with barefaced impunity.'

Thistlewood continues with a denunciation of Edwards: 'This Edwards, poor and penniless, lived near Pickett-street in the Strand, some time ago, without a bed to lie upon, or a chair to sit in. Straw was his resting-place; his only covering a blanket. Owing to his bad character, and his swindling conduct, he was driven from thence by his landlord. It is not my intention to trace him through his immorality: suffice it to say, that he was in every sense of the word a villain of the deepest atrocity. His landlord refused to give him a character Some short time after this, he called upon his landlord again; but mark the change in his appearance; dressed like a lord, in all the folly of the reigning fashion. He now described himself as the right heir to a German baron, who had been some time dead; that Lords Castlereagh and Sidmouth had acknowledged his claims to the title and property; had interfered in his behalf with the German government, and supplied him with money to support his rank in society. From this period I date his career as a government spy.'

He continues: 'Albion is still in chains of slavery. I quit it without regret. I shall be consigned to the grave, and my body will be immured beneath the soil whereon I first drew breath. My only sorrow is that that soil should be a theatre for slaves, for cowards and for despots. My motives, I doubt not, will hereafter be justly appreciated . . . The court decided upon my trial to commit murder rather than depart in the slightest degree from its usual forms; nay, it is with me question if the form is usual, which precluded me from examining witnesses . . . Ere the solicitor-general replied to the address of my counsel, I applied to the court to hear my witnesses: the court inhumanly [*sic*] refused, and I am in consequence to be consigned to the scaffold.'

Powerful stuff, if a touch flamboyantly worded.

Thistlewood was a revolutionary who had come to believe that only the working class could bring about its own freedom. Though middle class by upbringing, he would have scorned the middle-class reformers who then and for the rest of the nineteenth century dominated liberal and radical politics in this country. He aimed at a revolutionary coup d'etat to be followed by an appeal to the people. Action now was his belief. But it failed. He had misread the situation.

So there's these two Irish lads . . .

Up the close and doon the stair
But and ben' wi' Burke and Hare
Burke's the butcher, Hare's the thief,
Knox the boy that buys the beef.

A couple of hundred years or ago, the Resurrection Men – grave robbers
– were busy. Thank goodness, because when you think about it they
contributed greatly to the advances in medical science. That is not to
condone their activities: all that concerned these people were the coins
jangling in their pockets but, for the medical men and their students, how
ever could they really understand their work if they did not have the
opportunity to see in detail what lay under the skin? It doesn't seem too
absurd an analogy to compare them to garage workers who open the
bonnet of your car and really get down to the nitty-gritty, seeing what does
and what doesn't permit a proper functioning of the engine.

There were problems, however. Principally, there were insufficient
cadavers for students to work on. It's no good just having some lecturer
standing there giving an oral description of how the body operates: no
good simply hearing from him about the mechanics of the body. Surgeons
of the future needed bodies for dissection. The students needed to handle
the goods: the arms, legs, internal organs and so on. They were lacking
opportunities for practical work. But where were all these bodies to come
from?

In the old days the bodies of executed prisoners were practised on by
tyro surgeons, but in the 1800s, the period which interests us here, when
executed men and women were available to medical schools, no more than
an average of fifty-seven people were hanged each year. And of course,
there were the workhouse deaths and the unclaimed bodies of new-born
babies to add to the total. But none of it was enough as far as the education
of medics was concerned. The sad fact of all this is that at that time trainee
surgeons could not adequately learn their trade.

So what about the graveyards? What about those recently buried? All
that was needed was to dig them up. As long as they hadn't been too long
gone, as long as the corpse wasn't putrescent. If you could get a fresh corpse
there was good money in it. So along came the aforementioned Resurrection
Men, often with information about some poor, recently buried soul. They

could always get an accomplice to see where the plot of the recently buried was. They could find out if the family intended to watch over the grave for a few days or if they'd employed somebody else to stand guard. Maybe the coffin now underground was too secure for anyone to break it open in decent time, in which case they'd shun it, looking for an easier prize.

They needed good information if they were going to all the trouble of disinterring a body. And it wasn't easy, digging up a corpse with a wooden spade. Trouble was the metal spades made such a noise and you couldn't have that because it might alert a watchman. Mind you, selling corpses to hospitals paid well. In 1828, the year we're considering here, a good corpse, one with not too much fat on it, would bring £10. Now that was real money, worth something like £1,170 today.

So now let's introduce the two fellers who really made a name for themselves. During 1827 and 1828 two Irishmen, William Burke and William Hare, both former soldiers in their latish thirties and now resident in Edinburgh, developed a new strategy to the business of providing corpses to university anatomy lecturers. Quite out of nowhere, Burke and Hare – and it seems more likely than not, by the way, that they were both ably assisted by their womenfolk – came on the scene with their year-long, drink-fuelled murder spree, providing bodies for Dr Robert Knox, an immensely popular and much admired lecturer, at the University of Edinburgh.

The murder spree started, so it seems, relatively innocently enough. At Tanners Close, the lodging house that Hare owned – no, there is no indication of how such a feckless, booze-driven soul came to own a house – there was an elderly man named Donald who, when he died, owed Hare £4 in rent. Somehow, Hare heard that the university paid for bodies for teaching and research purposes. He talked the matter over with his lodger, Burke, and together they decided to fill the coffin with bark so that when the parish undertaker's men came to collect it they'd think the old feller was inside.

Then they called at the university and met Knox. He asked them to bring the goods after dark. No questions asked. After inspecting the body, Knox offered them £7 10s, about £750 at today's rate of exchange. Not a bad deal, the two scapegraces thought. When they talked it over there seemed to be some very promising business opportunities on the horizon.

There must've been some debate about another lodger, Joseph the miller, who apparently had a fever which couldn't be good for Hare's business. It wasn't as if he was dying. Not straightaway. Clearly he wasn't one of those who was going to last very long. So, why waste time? The two lads, they went to see him in his room and one of them pinched the old feller's nose and kept his mouth shut while, at the same time, his partner lay across the body, keeping the victim's arms and legs from flailing about, so that he couldn't put up much of a struggle.

And the way they'd carried out the whole business, when they'd finished with the old chap, there wasn't a mark on him. So they realised they'd struck on a really good way to polish off any likely candidate for the graveyard. And nobody could suspect that the old man had been done to death in any way. The author Lisa Rosner has offered the opinion that the method used would have been 'practically undetectable until the era of modern forensics'.

But frustratingly, Hare's tenants in general seemed to be resistant to illness. Despite the fact that their lives were probably seriously unhealthy, they didn't pass away frequently enough to provide the two Irishmen with a decent and regular income. So, perhaps reluctantly, the two of them concluded that they'd have to extend their hunting ground if they wanted extra prey. Hopeless cases that nobody would miss, these were just the sort of targets that suited Burke and Hare. They decided to select the kinds of people who just upped and died quite suddenly of natural causes, the sorts of death that people take as being normal.

What is unfortunate is that the chronology of the murders of Burke and Hare is so very uncertain. Perhaps in that half-drunk, half-dream land, in which they lived, they could neither of them later recapture times and dates with any accuracy. Perhaps even their two women, often as drink-sozzled as their menfolk, did not wish to reveal how intimate with the facts they really were or even how positively active they were in these gross affairs.

Let us assume, therefore, that it was in February of 1828 that Abigail Simpson, an elderly lady, was invited to spend the night in Hare's lodging house. It so happened that she was in Edinburgh only for a day to augment her pension with the sale of sea-salt. So the two men made merry with her and she was really drunk at the end of a lengthy session with the bottles. But then so were the two lads. In fact, they were so much with drink taken that they both passed out and slept till morning.

Anyway, next day the old lady is up bright and early and ready for the off. 'Got a hangover, have you?' Burke asks her. 'Well, here's the cure.' And he hands her another generous glass of whisky and she knocks it back. What a good start to her day, she must be thinking. And she really likes the stuff and so she has another and later they kill her with their usual enthusiasm, in the same manner they had used on Joseph the miller. When they met him later in the day, Dr Knox was delighted to be offered such an extremely fresh piece of merchandise, and he handed over £10 very cheerfully.

The next victim, known simply as 'the Englishman', was a match seller. While lodging with the Hares he fell ill, poor chap, and was attended to in the Burke and Hare style and his body was sold without any questions.

Then Margaret Hare, who later was to claim complete ignorance of these matters, gets into the act and persuades an unnamed lady into staying with them. Not only that, but the two women set to on a bottle of Scotch and eventually the guest is very drunk. At this point the two men are summoned and, according to Margaret's account, she left them with the unconscious woman. And we know what happened next …

In April, an eighteen-year-old prostitute, Mary Patterson, along with her friend, Janet Brown, met Burke quite by chance in Canongate and he invited them along to Tanners Close, 'to have a couple of drinks, eh?' After a while Janet Brown, lucky girl, left her friend as she had some other kind of business to attend to. But later she didn't meet up with Mary as she had expected so she went back to Hare's place. Apparently, according to Hare, Mary had just gone out with Burke.

'You've just missed her,' she was told. 'She'll be back soon. You can wait and maybe have a wee drink.' So Janet decided to wait. This nearly cost her her life. However, Janet's landlady, after learning that Mary Patterson was missing, was concerned about her and sent her servant to find her. So Janet was rescued at the last minute. Later, the story circulated, encouraged no doubt by certain parties, that Mary had come to no harm, She'd gone off to live in Glasgow with a travelling salesman. So it was said.

Despite the fact that several of the medical students knew Mary, having previously hired her services, no news of her body being sold and dissected, leaked out. Janet was not told by anyone what had happened to her friend, despite her frequently enquiring around town. Perhaps there were several students who met her on the dissecting table and who recognised her but said nothing. This arrangement in the medical school was surely an open secret.

And now another woman known as Effie, 'a cinder gatherer', comes briefly on the scene. She's known Burke from the time when he was a cobbler and she was selling leather. Now Burke tells her he's interested in some leather if she has some available and he invites her across to Tanners Close. Such hospitality. Such stomach-churning callousness.

Then there was a drunk, a woman who could scarcely stand up and who was in the process of being arrested by police and taken to the cells until she sobered up. Quite by chance, Burke happened to be on the scene. Pretending to know her, Burke convinced the policeman to hand her over to him. He'd take her home, he said. And he did, and later Dr Knox handed over £10.

In June 1828, Burke met an old woman in the street along with her deaf and physically handicapped teenage grandson. Just her bad luck to stop and ask him for directions to some or other place. No bother for me, Burke probably said. In fact, he was going that way himself and he'd accompany them with pleasure. And you know, kind chap that he appeared to be, he invited them into the place where he lived. They could have some refreshment and a rest before continuing their way. So out comes the whisky for the old lady, and Burke, he's generous with it.

But she takes too much and she's quite overcome, poor soul. And later still, she's smothered while her grandson is being entertained in another room by Helen and Margaret who've been trying to get him to take drink with them. Why not, he's grown up, isn't he? And having a drink, that's what real men do. But he refuses. He doesn't like it, he tells them. He'd rather have a cup of tea. Well, this is a problem for the two fellers who've just killed his grannie. What are they going to do with him? Let him go? With the old lady lying in the next room? How are they going to explain to the lad about his grannie?

So they decided it might on balance be best for them to murder him as well. But he still won't take a drink. It's ridiculous, a lad his age. But there's nothing for it but to attack him which they did very violently, so violently in fact that they broke his back. Then the usual tea chest wasn't large enough to hold two corpses so they had to force them into larger herring barrel. The two bodies sold for £16 and amazing, really, nobody at the hospital seemed to notice he had a broken back. Or perhaps they did notice but decided that wasn't worth enquiring about.

Mrs Ostler, a washerwoman, stayed at the house very briefly, just long enough to be prepared and sold. Then there was also a woman called Ann who also stayed for a short while. She was, in fact, related to Helen McDougal, Burke's mistress. Consequently, out of delicacy, Burke did not participate in this murder for which Hare received £10.

Mary Haldane, described as 'a stout old woman', was a prostitute whom Hare invited back to the lodging house and, as ever, got her drunk and she was smothered. Peggy Haldane was Mary Haldane's daughter who several months later heard some tale about her mother and the Irish fellers so she sought them out at Hare's lodging house. But when she arrived the two men denied that Mary had ever been there, saying they didn't take in prostitutes. In any event, as a courtesy, they invited Peggy in for a drink. You couldn't do less for a girl looking for her mother. They got her drunk and murdered her and took the body off to Dr Knox in the tea chest.

Then there was poor Jamie Wilson, an 18-year-old, a mentally retarded boy who was crippled. 'Daft Jamie' was well known and very popular in the city. He told jokes and stories to children for a few pennies. In October of 1828 Hare decided to target the youth. One day Jamie asked him if he had seen his mother. He couldn't find her. Hare said he thought he could help him and invited him home with the usual outcome, though not without a struggle as Jamie, unlike the other victims, was more or less a non-drinker. He was a snuff-taker, that was his little indulgence.

Then when Jamie's body was in the medical quarters he was recognised by some of Dr Knox's students. The doctor's response was to cut off the boy's head and his deformed feet so that he could not be easily identified.

Anyway, the two men came away with the usual fee plus Jamie's snuff box, kept by Burke, and the snuff spoon, which Hare hung on to.

The final victim, Mary Docherty, an Irish woman, was lured into the lodging house by Burke. When he heard her name, he told her that his mother was a Docherty and that they were probably relatives. Such smooth patter, such cynical comment.

Mary was not murdered straightaway because the Grays, their fellow lodgers, who were unaware of the activities of the Irishmen, were in the house. Later these two young folks were persuaded, by some totally specious reason, to sleep elsewhere that night. It would only be a temporary arrangement, they were told. So they agreed. After all, Mary was Burke's relative, wasn't she?

The following day, the Grays returned to Tanners Close, intending to pick up a pair of stockings that Ann had left in their room. All sorts of difficulties were advanced and they were refused admission to their quarters. It was inconvenient, so they were told. Later in the day, if they'd come back, it'd be all right. But not now. It's unclear how the Grays eventually effected entry to their room: had the Burkes as well as the Hares gone out? Anyway, in the room they found Mary Docherty's body under the bed, blood and saliva on her face,. They straightaway went to the police.

On the way there they ran into Helen McDougal, who started bargaining. 'Don't go to the police and we'll give you ten shillings a week.' For how long? For life? But life doesn't always last long, does it? The Grays wouldn't change their minds.

Before the police arrived, Burke and Hare, warned by Helen, had removed the body, but they had been seen carrying a large tea chest from the house. Dr Knox's porter also confirmed later that Mrs Docherty's body was brought in a tea-chest. In any event, at the beginning, the police had little direct evidence. For a start, there was no body in the house. Only when interrogated, did the stories of Burke and Helen McDougal fail to match. Asked when Mary Docherty left the house, one said 7am and the other 7pm. And then the police discovered Mary's body in Dr Knox's surgery.

Such a furore. What a great story for the newspapers. As a result of the publicity, other people came forward to speak, not only of missing people but also the names of Burke and Hare kept cropping up. Even so, because there was very little direct evidence that the two had actually murdered anyone, the case against them wasn't particularly strong.

And what of their women? Helen McDougal and Margaret Hare – had they actually been involved directly? Did they even know what, if anything, had been going on in the house? No, they claimed ignorance. But, according to Burke at the trial, Margaret Hare had suggested that they kill Helen McDougal as 'they could not trust her, as she was a Scotch woman'. Burke had strongly objected and there was a temporary rift in the relationship of the two men.

Determined to crack this case, made so difficult because of the lack of direct evidence, the lord advocate took a stance, though it is not clear how he justified his decision. He opined that Burke had been the leader and so offered Hare, were he sufficiently helfpul, full immunity. Well, it was a way of going forward.

One of two accused of the most gory, the most sickening crimes, was given what was in effect a pre-trial pardon. All Hare needed do to walk free was to confess his part in the matter and then go in the witness box and give evidence against Burke, a man whom we must assume was a friend.

Hare readily accepted the deal, and as a bonus he offered information implicating Helen McDougal. In addition, he made a comment about Dr Knox, saying that he 'never encouraged him to murder any person'.

Burke they did convict, but he immediately cleared Helen, claiming that she knew nothing whatsoever of the murders. Whether guilty or not, there was a strong belief that Helen had been involved, but as it could not be directly proven, the jury was forced to release her. When the verdict was announced Burke was reportedly overjoyed that Helen was free. For the first time in this loathsome tale there's a hint of genuine human feeling for another person.

Just over a month later William Burke was hanged. Seats with a view of the gallows apparently went for excessively high fees. And Burke, seeing and hearing the crowd yelling at him, rushed to the noose trying to speed up the whole awful operation. As custom and the law demanded, after a two-minute struggle at the end of the rope, his corpse was removed while the frenzied crowd tried in its usual unseemly way to cut off pieces of the rope as souvenirs of their day out. Had they had access to Burke they would have torn him apart.

Burke's body, however,was taken for dissection, which was performed publicly by Professor Monro. Was this to deter the masses? Or to give some kind of esoteric thrill? During the two-hour procedure, this man of superior education, this man of more refined sensibilities, dipped his quill pen into Burke's blood and wrote on the official document: 'This is written with the blood of Wm Burke, who was hanged at Edinburgh. This blood was taken from his head.'

So how does it end? Dr Knox, declared in court to be 'deficient in principle and heart', did not suffer any legal punishment, but he certainly fell from grace. Many people believed that he was 'a sinister ringmaster who got Burke and Hare dancing to his tune'. Disgraced, he eventually quit Edinburgh and its university and went to London to continue his medical work. The two women, Helen McDougal and Margaret Hare, wherever they went in Edinburgh, met angry, threatening crowds and both soon left Scotland. As for Hare, he was last seen being menaced by a crowd and rescued by police. Then, rather like the two ladies, he disappeared.

And out of it all the 1832 Anatomy Act was passed, greatly increasing the legal supply of cadavers. From now it was possible for doctors, lecturers and medical students to dissect donated bodies. No need for murder any more.

It's a Family Matter

Happiness is having a large, loving, caring, close-knit family – in another city.

George Burns

George Bodle's substantial farm, Montague House, situated in the High Street, is extensive, with fine barns and granaries. His house is surrounded by well-tended hedges. At the side of the house runs a cart track, overhung with apple trees, heavy with blossom in spring and, in summer, laden with fruit. By the roadside there is a kitchen garden where these days the old man potters. A stream runs through a pond at the rear of the house. Here is the orchard at the end of which a gate leads to a cottage where Mr Bodle's son John lives with his wife and two sons, George and Young John. Years earlier, during the Napoleonic wars, like many farmers, George Bodle made a considerable amount of money and now the 80-year-old, a church-warden, is well known and highly respected in the district.

It is idyllic here. It is Plumstead. It is 1833. And George Bodle, in today's terms, is a millionaire. But it is no longer summer now. Autumn trails its way out and it's dark, this second day of November. Even so, at six o'clock in the morning, there is a bustle about the place. Several of the servants sleep in the house and already they are at work by candlelight. Henry Parker, the cowboy (so he is described) is off to bring in the cattle for milking. Sophia Taylor, a Foots Cray girl, has already lit the fire and is now cleaning the stove. Shortly, she will have to set about making the breakfasts. Then there will be the churning to do and the preparing of the meals for the rest of the day. Of course, Elizabeth Smith, the deaf and dumb girl, is there to help her with the day's chores and so is old Mrs Leah who does some of the cleaning. And, fortunately, Mrs Elizabeth Evans, Mrs Bodle's daughter from her first marriage, has been staying for the past three days and she can be quite helpful.

Then Young John Bodle breezes in this Saturday morning and, on seeing Sophia on her knees at the stove, asks if there's anything he can do to help.

'Nothing that I know of,' Sophia tells him, but there's so much to do and it's kind of him to ask, she thinks. It always gets the day off to a good start when Young John arrives with his cans to collect the milk for his family. For the past fortnight, he has come down every morning early, sat himself down and talked and sometimes has made himself useful in small ways. He is such fun and he tells jokes and there was the time when he even dressed up in women's clothes and made them all laugh. Sophia really enjoys it when he comes, and so does Elizabeth Smith. And they have a kind of flirtatious relationship, Sophia and Young John, and they play the odd daft trick on each other. It helps in the mornings. After all, she is only 20 and he is just 22.

Sophia goes down to the cellar for the milk while he opens the window shutters in the kitchen and the wash-house for her. Then he goes out to the pump in the yard, just outside the kitchen door, and fills the great iron kettle. It's usually Henry Parker's task but he is with the cattle this morning so Young John has offered to do it. And when Sophia comes back, there's the kettle already hanging over the fire.

Shortly after this, Young John leaves with his cans of milk. When the kettle boils, Sophia fills the coffee pot and serves Mr Bodle's breakfast downstairs. Elizabeth Evans takes coffee and toast upstairs to her mother, who is unwell. The old people's immediate needs attended to, Mrs Evans, Elizabeth Smith and Sophia breakfast together. They use the same coffee pot, just adding more boiling water.

Half an hour after breakfast Sophia meets Mr Bodle in the yard. He's been feeding the hens. She tells him she has just been very sick. She feels dreadful. So does he, he says. He's been sick too. She's had two cups of coffee and wonders if that might be the cause.

In the course of the day the whole household is laid low. Elizabeth Smith is violently ill as is Elizabeth Evans. Like the rest, old Mrs Bodle, already under the weather, is constantly vomiting, suffering severe attacks of diarrhoea. Only Henry Parker seems to have escaped. But he didn't have breakfast with the rest. He is called upon for the rest of the day to help with quite unfamiliar duties in the house. Fortunately, Mrs Leah, the charwoman, is also unaffected. She has been lucky because, as usual, she was given the coffee grounds to take home but when her daughter looked at what her mother had brought she had thought they seemed unusually thick and didn't use them.

Stomach upsets are not unusual in this pre-Victorian world. People suffer but they usually recover. But by late afternoon the Bodle family and their servants are becoming concerned for themselves, all of them labouring under the same wretched symptoms. They wonder if they have caught cholera.

Dr Butler is summoned from Woolwich. On arrival at Montague House, he finds George Bodle in a serious condition. The old man has been violently sick eight or nine times and has acute stomach pains. He is intensely thirsty and has a burning sensation in the throat. The doctor asks everyone what they have had for breakfast and the common factor seems to be the coffee or the water. Mrs Leah has brought back the coffee grounds she took home and the doctor takes them with him when he leaves. He goes to Woolwich, handing over the grounds to Mr Marsh, a 'practical chemist' at the Royal Arsenal. Perhaps the kettle, too, would have provided further information had not Henry Parker been instructed by old Mr Bodle to scrape it out thoroughly with a chisel in case it had been the cause of their illness.

Over the next day or so most of the patients recover at varying rates, although Sophia Taylor will be confined to bed for much of the following week. Only George Bodle's condition gives cause for concern. Still suffering greatly and fearing that the water might be contaminated, he calls for a pint of ale. According to the doctor, it is this in part which prevents his recovery. George Bodle dies on the Tuesday. His body is examined by the doctor and two of his colleagues. The stomach is inflamed but it is the condition of the other organs that tells them definitely that the old man has died of arsenic poisoning. Mr Marsh confirms the presence of arsenic in the coffee pot, though whether it was the water or the coffee itself will never be cleared up

Is this a deliberate poisoning? And if so, if there are suspicions, on whom do they fall? Of all people, Young John Bodle seems the likely candidate because, and it seems almost out of the blue, he has left Plumstead at a time when his grandfather is dying; when his grandmother is still sick; when the girls he has chaffed and joked with in recent days are ill. Is this not odd? Doesn't it seem callous? But it's unthinkable, the idea of Young John poisoning anybody.

On Wednesday the magistrates received confidential information that seems further to point at Young John as the poisoner. It is his own father who carries this information to the magistrates. His son, he says, is guilty. And he mentions his wife, Young John's mother, as party to an incriminating conversation. John Bodle has also told the investigators about his servant, Mary Higgins, who overheard only a week ago some strange words.

According to Mary Higgins, Mrs John Bodle had said, 'John, I wish your father was dead.'

And Young John had answered, 'I wish that grandfather was dead.'

His grandfather? Why?

'Because we shall have thousands a year,' he had said.

Are such thoughts usually aired so openly in front of the servants? For that matter, are they expressed so openly in front of anyone? Perhaps if the conversation did take place, it was all in jest. At the time Mary Higgins had not taken the conversation seriously. But now, given the circumstances…

And given the information from the analyst, Mr Marsh, that there was arsenic in the pot …

And also the further information that Young John has twice in recent weeks purchased arsenic locally, there is need to send for him wherever he might be. He must be arrested at once. Arsenic, indeed. That's the poison the French called the 'inheritance powder'.

Constable Morris, with a warrant for his arrest, is told where his quarry is. Young John has gone off to Clerkenwell, to his sister's house, and it is there that he is arrested on the Wednesday.

'You can't want me,' he protests. 'It must be my brother George you want.'

At this point he faints and Morris handcuffs him. Later the pair travel back to Plumstead by horse-drawn public omnibus. At Plumstead he is confined in the local lock-up.

Now Young John tells the constable that he will find two packages and a bottle in his trunk at home. Morris collects what is surely valuable evidence although he has a misfortune with the bottle which he drops. He was to explain that the accident happened while he was bending down to fasten his shoe laces but his superiors believe him to have taken too much alcohol in the course of his busy day and he is placed under suspension. Nevertheless, the two packets are intact and they do contain arsenic.

Can Young John Bodle really have poisoned his grandfather? The inquest was held on the Thursday at the Plume of Feathers tavern in Plumstead. All of those concerned give evidence: Dr Butler; Sophia Taylor (from her bed, for she was unfit to attend); Elizabeth Evans; Henry Parker, the cowboy; Elizabeth Smith, the deaf and dumb girl, speaking through an interpreter; Mary Higgins whose master, John Bodle, had told her to tell all she knew; Mr Marsh, the 'practical chemist'; and others who had witnessed Young John's purchase of the arsenic. Why should he have bought arsenic? Why was such a quantity of the poison found among his possessions? Was that not a clear enough indication of his intentions?

And motive? It was stated that George Bodle had made his will only a fortnight earlier although the disposition of his property was not stated. Perhaps the young man was trying to advance matters. Then it transpired that before the old man died, he had taken an affectionate leave of his son but had forbidden Young John access. Did George Bodle believe that his grandson had poisoned him?

Even so, there were those who spoke so warmly of Young John. Sophia Taylor could not entertain the idea that he, John, had attempted to poison her. She had known him since she came to work for Mr and Mrs Bodle two-and-a-half years earlier and had always been on good terms with him. 'He's a nice young man and I have nothing to say against him,' she insisted. Mrs Elizabeth Smith seemed to think that it was the absent Henry Parker who put the kettle on that morning – so frail are our memories for such ordinary daily details – and agreed that Young John was a very good lad, always ready to lend a hand. As for Henry Parker, he was sure that the kettle was already filled when he came in but could not say who put it on the fire.

Eventually, the coroner's jury reached a verdict of wilful murder and Young John Bodle was committed to trial.

By the time the Maidstone Assizes opened on 12 December 1833 there was a swell of local sympathy in favour of the prisoner. Many in the jam-packed courtroom sympathised with the accused, sitting in the dock, 'dressed very genteel in deep mourning'. In spite of all that had been said there were still many doubts surrounding the case. If anyone in the family could contemplate murder, surely Young John was the last one you'd think of. But his father, what about him? That notorious philanderer, mightn't he have need of money? But was it likely that a father could condemn his own son unless there was some truth in the accusation? And so the rumours circulated.

There was the usual army of witnesses, repeating more or less what they had already recited at the inquest. Elizabeth Smith's sign-reader explained that the girl was certain that Young John put the kettle on. For his part, however, Henry Parker was unable to remember saying at the inquest that he found the kettle filled and someone else had put it on the fire. He was now certain that he himself had put the kettle on. But that was until he again became uncertain about the matter. Had he not been with the cattle?

Dr Butler was lucid enough in the witness box but crucially he was unable to clarify whether the poison had been put into the kettle or mixed with the coffee grounds. This was important: there was no suggestion that Young John had been near the coffee jar which was kept locked away in a cupboard.

The apothecary, Joseph Evans, clearly recalled selling arsenic on two occasions to Young John. But he had not questioned the purchase. Plenty of people bought arsenic from him. If people did not keep a cat, or if they did not care to set traps for rats, they laid down arsenic. There was nothing out of the ordinary in buying arsenic and, until the present matter, Evans had not given the slightest thought to the fact that Young John had purchased arsenic from him.

Sophia Taylor went quite confidently through the oft-repeated tale of what happened in the kitchen on the morning of the poisoning. Then she was asked a question she could not answer. She had never heard that Old John Bodle had recently been forbidden entry to his father's house. And no, she said in answer to further little probing queries, she had never known a woman called Hodges. Nor anyone called Mrs Shears nor yet another named Warwickshire. Nor had she ever heard of a Mrs Warren. Who were these? some of those in court must have wondered. Ah yes, well, John Bodle had a reputation for liking the ladies.

As for Elizabeth Evans, she had never heard of Old John Bodle being banned from his father's house. This is an interesting area which was not resolved at the trial. It is unclear still if and why and for what reason he was denied access to the house. Certainly he was there at his father's bedside when he died and there is evidence that he went to the house to deal with farm matters. Perhaps George Bodle simply refused to meet his dissolute son socially.

More intriguing stuff came from Mrs Leah, some of which may clarify the old man's displeasure with his son. Though it seems on the face of it to have little to do with the death of George Bodle there may be some pointers to a kind of secret history. Mrs Leah was asked if she knew a woman called Hodges living in Plumstead. Yes, she did, but no, she did not know that Old John Bodle had been living with her and that he had children by her. Also, while she also knew a woman named Stevenson living at Shoulder of Mutton Green, only a couple of miles from Plumstead, she did not know that she had a family by John Bodle. And she expressed ignorance of any woman called Warwickshire.

How long had she known Mr John Bodle, Mrs Leah was asked. Several years, she said, but the judge now hurriedly intervened. This questioning was leading nowhere and so we shall never find the answer to 'Did you not know him in Maidstone jail?' Secret history indeed.

Then comes Mary Higgins who had gone with her master, John Bodle, to the magistrate the day after his father's death. She gives some unexceptional information about what occurred in John Bodle's kitchen on the morning of the poisoning. The routines were identical to those of the farmhouse only fifty yards or so away. He'd got up before six o'clock and just like Sophie and Elizabeth up at the big house, Mary had busied herself lighting the fire, taking down the shutters and so on. She remembered Young John was up unusually early that morning and recalled his going to the farmhouse with the milk cans.

But it was the conversations that she had overheard that intrigued the court. She repeated the account that she had earlier given to the coroner's court and the magistrates. She told how she heard Mrs Bodle and her son, Young John, talking together in the kitchen and how Mrs Bodle had said that she wished her husband was dead. Apparently that hadn't caused Young John any surprise and he'd gone on to say that he wished his grandfather were dead. And the succeeding talk was all about money.

But even more dramatically, she spoke about Young John and his mother talking in the kitchen at about three o'clock on the Saturday afternoon. Old Mr Bodle and his wife, Mrs Evans and the servants were now all laid low. Young John had said to his mother that he would not mind poisoning anyone that he did not like. That was silly talk, his mother had told him. And he had replied, 'Only give me the stuff and you'll see.' His mother answered that she wouldn't risk her own soul into danger for anyone.

On the second day of the trial, the ladies man John Bodle was in the witness box, and, although he disagreed with some of Mary Higgins's testimony, he remembered her telling him she had heard Young John remark that 'he had done for one party and would do for another and that he was satisfied with what he had done'. Was this just Young John fooling about?

Under cross-examination Bodle said, 'I believe I'm entitled to have the bulk of my father's property after the death of my mother. I've never heard that he altered his will shortly before his death.'

But then John was rattled by the more probing questions about his personal life. 'I object to answering whether I have ever been charged with a felony or that I have ever been in Maidstone jail or that I have families living by three different women besides my wife, or that I was ever charged with attempting to cut my wife's throat.'

That's an awful amount of personal history for a man to have to deny. This line of enquiry was stopped when the judge intervened, but serious damage had been done to the prosecution case. By the time he left the witness box some wondered whether Old John Bodle was the more likely to be the guilty party.

Then came the opportunity to hear Young John's side of things. At that time, counsel was not permitted to address the jury on behalf of clients. In his defence, Young John handed in a long, handwritten statement, which was read aloud by the clerk of the court. This document had been composed, under the prisoner's instructions, by his counsel, the solicitor, Mr Colquhoun. It was a skilful declaration and made a strong impression. Most powerful is the way in which Young John deals with his father who had gone to the magistrates with false information.

'My father is the first person to accuse me of this crime. It is he who has encouraged Mary Higgins as a witness to procure my condemnation. What can be the motive which has induced a father thus to conduct himself towards his child? Gentlemen, I grieve to say my father has not set a fit and worthy example before his family. It has been a lot of his children to see him imprisoned for malicious injury and guilty of profligacy of all kinds, but still the voice of nature cannot be dead within him. What is his overwhelming motive? Can any adequate reason be suggested except the desire to avert from himself the terrible consequences of this horrible offence? What a light does not this throw upon the whole mystery! My father had the run of the house and in his anxiety to throw suspicion from himself, he eagerly accuses his own child, misrepresenting facts, swearing to a fabricated conversation with his servant, and exhibiting a line of conduct wicked, unnatural and irreconcilable except by the dreadful explanation I suggest.'

Old John Bodle might have been denied access to his father but he had 'the run of the house'; he could roam the farmhouse, perhaps before anyone else rose. It gave him ample opportunity to poison the coffee.

As for Young John's absconding from home, there was no mystery about that. He had been invited to Clerkenwell by his sister and he had gone on the Tuesday, believing the worst effects of the poisoning were over. He did not know that his grandfather was on the point of dying.

And the arsenic he had bought? What about that? He explained that some years earlier he had the misfortune to be subject to an attack of 'the itch', brought into the family by his father who had been cohabiting with a Mrs Warren. As a cure he used a mixture of arsenic and hellebore, a well-known remedy for what seems to have been syphilis. He had tried to keep quiet about it. But there was a witness to his ailment, Mrs Perks, a former landlady, who would testify that while he lived in her house at Shoreditch he had always kept arsenic in his trunk. To alleviate his condition, he used to mix arsenic with lard.

Reverting to the evidence of his father and Mary Higgins, Young John says 'I feel I should be insulting your judgement if I thought you could believe one syllable of their story. You will recollect that my own father is the first person to accuse me of this dreadful crime. He it is who goes to the magistrate and puts this charge in motion against me. He it is who, after an interview with Mary Higgins, produces her as a witness to ensure my condemnation, by swearing to a conversation that never occurred, and in the relation of which they falter and equivocate in the manner you have heard.'

What, he asks, could induce someone to become 'not only the willing accuser of his child but the fabricator of false evidence against him?'

It was a highly effective defence.

Finally, the judge began to sum up, but he was interrupted by the jury foreman. The jury apparently had already resolved to find a prisoner not guilty. There was no need for his lordship to outline the pros and cons.

And so, to immense excitement, to loud the applause and cheers and some tears of relief, Young John Bodle left the court, waving as he went. Outside, he was received with open arms by his grandmother. All of the jurymen shook him by the hand. Back in Plumstead, the whole village turned out to welcome him home. The following Sunday, when he attended church, special thanks during prayers were offered for his delivery.

The case was never followed up. No charges were laid against Old John Bodle or Mary Higgins, though for long years people had their own ideas of what had happened.

Postscript
Tuesday 14 March 1844
CONVICTS FOR VAN DIEMENS LAND.The London hired convict ship, at present moored off the dockyard, Woolwich, has already on board 244 convicts from the Millbank Penitentiary, the Model Prison, Pentonville, and from several country gaols, and is expected to take out in all about 300 of that unfortunate class, who will be guarded by detachments of the 58th

and 80th Regiments . . . Amongst the convict prisoners on board the London is the well-known character in Plumstead and Woolwich, named John Bodle, who was found guilty at the last Central Criminal Court sessions, and sentenced to twenty years' transportation for endeavouring to extort money from Lord Abingdon's butler, under a threat, if he did not comply with his demands, of charging him with an unnatural crime. Since the prisoner's conviction for this offence he has confessed having poisoned his grandfather, although he was tried at Maidstone on that charge, but acquitted. Several of his relations applied yesterday at the Woolwich dockyard for permission to visit the prisoner previous to his leaving the country for the long period named in his sentence. (*Morning Post*)

The Fortune Hunters

When the Fox hears the Rabbit scream he comes a-runnin', but not to help.

Thomas Harris

Poor Harriet Butterfield never had a suitor until she was in her mid-thirties. So why, when one finally did come along, did her mother try to stop her marrying him? It seemed so unfair to Harriet – so unfair, in fact, that off she went to live with an aunt. Her mother then tried to have her committed as a lunatic – and failed. Then she tried to have he made a ward in Chancery – and failed again.

What motivated Mrs Butterfield? Did she fear that young Lewis Staunton was after her daughter's fortune? The first Married Women's Property Act had been passed only shortly before to prevent that sort of thing. Did she think that Lewis had found a loophole?

In spite of her mother, in June 1875, Harriet married Lewis, an auctioneers clerk aged twenty-four, ten years her junior.

Mrs Butterfield went on worrying. She knew her daughter was of very weak intellect, quite incapable of managing her own affairs. Swallowing her pride, three weeks after the wedding, she paid the young couple a visit at their home at 8 Loughborough Road, Brixton. She stayed only quarter of an hour but nevertheless they parted, as she thought, on reasonable terms.

The following day, however, Mrs Butterfield received a letter from Lewis Staunton forbidding her from calling at the house and denying her any further contact with her daughter. A note from Harriet supported her husband. Mrs Butterfield was never to see Harriet again.

Later in the year, when Harriet became pregnant, twenty-year-old Alice Rhodes came to live at Loughborough Road. Alice's sister, Lizzie, was married to Lewis's brother, Patrick. Ostensibly, she had come to help Harriet during her pregnancy. In truth, she had been Lewis's mistress before his marriage and was to remain so. Clara Brown, a sixteen-year-old, who acted as a servant to her two cousins, Alice and Lizzie, was also at Loughborough Road for some of the time. She said later that Lewis and Alice showed each other a great deal more than affection than was necessary.

Mrs Butterfield's suspicions about her son-in-law's motives for marrying Harriet had certainly been correct. In March 1876, the couple's son,

Thomas Henry Staunton, was born. More important to Lewis, however, was the fact that £1,177 15 shillings and 2d was transferred into his own bank account from Harriet's trust fund. In the next month £639 4 shillings and 1d took the same route, followed in June by £310 4 shillings and 6d. And there was more to come.

Perhaps it was because Harriet could not adequately care for the child that Tommy was sent to live with Lewis's younger brother, Patrick, a professional artist, and his wife Lizzie. They had recently moved from Brixton to the remote and beautiful village of Cudham, near Bromley. Here their two-up, two-down cottage, Woodlands, lay well back from the road, the rear and sides of the dwelling being heavily wooded. The nearest of their very few neighbours were three hundred yards away. Young Clara Brown was there much of the time and Lewis often stayed there, sometimes with Alice, occasionally with his wife, Harriet.

Lewis was busy. Using his wife's money he had established himself as an auctioneer in Gypsy Hill, where he and Harriet now moved. But what ought to have been for the young man an exciting time, with a new baby and a new business, he found less than congenial. A letter written in late June 1876 to Patrick – he calls him 'Bay', by the way – gives an indication of this:

'No one knows, my dear Bay, what I have had to put up with from Harriet the last six months. Her temper has been something frightful. I have talked to her for hours together and tried to reason with her but it is all of no use. From the time she gets up in the morning until she goes to bed at night she does nothing but aggravate and make me as miserable as she possibly can . . . I have been disheartened and cried for hours to think I should have laid out money to make things nice and have no one to take any interest in the place. I am, indeed, truly unhappy.'

Even if Harriet had on occasion a bad temper – and there is some evidence of this – Lewis should have remembered that most of his money came from her; that competent mother or no, her child had gone from her and it was apparent even to her that something was going on between Alice and Lewis.

Sometime in August Harriet went to stay at Woodlands. But perhaps Patrick and Lizzie, too, found her a trial at times. A letter from Lewis dated 28th August refers to Patrick's two dear children who are ill and goes on, 'I want you to send Harriet up tomorrow, for I am sure you cannot be bothered with her just now,' he writes, 'but I will then send Alice down to help dear Lizzy.' Certainly Lewis seems to have had some affection for his brother's wife and children.

Three days later, Harriet was still at Cudham – in fact, she was never to leave – and Lewis was apologising to Patrick again: 'I feel so sorry Harriet should have given you so much trouble. What to do with her I do not know.'

At this time Lewis was paying his brother one pound a week for Harriet's keep. She stayed on, tolerated, lonely, seeing her husband some weekends. A letter from her in September suggests her loneliness and her hope of returning home to Gypsy Hill. The letter hints, too, at some domestic casualness.

'My own darling, I write these few lines hoping they will find you well. Will you be down on Sunday? If not I shall be disappointed. Hope to see you on Monday. If not let me know which day you will be down. Will you bring me down please peace [sic] ribon (sic) and frilling for my colour [sic] and selves [sleeves]. I hope to return to town with you soon. Tommy is quite well, so good night, my dear, God bless you. I have not had a clean flannel for a month on Saturday. It is time I shall be at home. My boots has worn out. From your ever affectionate wife, Harriet.'

Harriet continued to dream of the day when she and Tommy would return to Gypsy Hill, unaware that in October Lewis had sold the Gypsy

Hill business and moved to Little Gray's Farm, only a mile from Woodlands. Alice, now pregnant, moved in with him, passing herself off as his wife. Patrick and Lizzie played their part in this deception. Had they conspired, all of them, and determined a way out for Lewis? After all, he now had most of his wife's property – there was just one more transaction to make, after which time she would be no more to them than an obstacle and a nuisance.

A bequest to Harriet of £2,000 was to be made over to Lewis and it was necessary that this be done legally before a commissioner in London. As a married woman she could only dispose of her property if the commissioner was satisfied that she was doing so of her own free will.

For Harriet, then, there were a couple of outings to London with Lewis. On their visit on 17 October she was in such a nervous state that the negotiation could not be completed. All was satisfactory on the visit on 23 October, however, when she signed away the last of her fortune, although the commissioner was later to admit that he had been slightly worried about bruises around Harriet's eyes.

Then came a new and final phase in the life of Harriet Staunton. From now on she was rarely seen. Between October 1876 and April 1877 only two people outside the family, a gamekeeper and a visiting fishmonger, caught sight of her. At Christmas time two girls who called at the house heard her footsteps in the kitchen but did not see her. None of these people, however, had any knowledge of who she was.

Over Christmas, Harriet and Tommy were left in the care of young Clara Brown. Patrick and Lizzie were away for several days; Lewis did not come to see his wife and child. She made no effort to leave Woodlands, presumably by now accepting that she was to stay there.

After Christmas, Harriet no longer joined the others downstairs. She was confined to a bedroom, 13' 2" by 8' 2", which she shared with Clara, Tommy and one of Patrick's babies. Clara was to relate in court how Patrick, a vicious young man, once called out to her, 'You mustn't come downstairs or I'll break your neck.'

In February 1877 Mrs Butterfield, who had written without success to Lewis, managed to meet Alice Rhodes at London Bridge station. Alice was not especially helpful; after all, her lover hated Harriet's mother. She first told Mrs Butterfield she did not know where Harriet was and later told her he was with Lewis in Brighton. Her daughter was happy, Mrs Butterfield was told. 'You should see her playing with little Tommy. It is great fun.'

But it was not great fun. By then Harriet was increasingly incapable of playing with Tommy. And Tommy was increasingly incapable of being played with.

Mrs Butterfield persevered, still hoping to see her daughter. She also met Patrick at London Bridge station, but he threatened her. 'If you come to my house,' he told her, 'I'll blow your brains out.'

Undeterred, the old woman made her way to Cudham, arriving at Little Gray's Farm where she believed Harriet to be. Lewis refused her entry. 'If you would only let me hear her voice or see her hand on the balustrade,' she pleaded, 'I should know that she was in her proper place.'

'You will never see her if you live a thousand years,' her son-in-law told her.

Mrs Butterfield next asked the local police to watch Little Gray's Farm and report any sign of Harriet to her. They did keep a watch for some weeks but naturally, as Harriet was at Woodlands, they were unable to offer her mother any comforting news.

Matters came to a head shortly afterwards. On 10th April, Patrick and Lizzie took Tommy into Guy's Hospital. Lewis stayed outside. They told the nurse the child was ill, the mother being incapable of looking after him. Little Tommy, a year old now, was wearing the clothes of the month-old child. Patrick returned to the hospital the next day with appropriate clothing, to learn the Tommy had died. Of starvation.

Lewis, now using the name John Harris and claiming to be acting on behalf of the child's family, arranged the funeral. He did not want it to be expensive, he said. The child's name was entered in the register as Henry Stornton.

The following day, 12 April, it was decided that something had to be done about Harriet who was by now too ill to comprehend that her baby was dead. A druggist at Westerham refused to prescribe medicine, advising them to see a doctor. Instead, Lewis, Patrick and Lizzie immediately left Harriet in the care of Alice while they went by train from Bromley to Penge where they rented two rooms in Forbes Road. Here they told the landlady, Mrs Chalkin, that later in the day they would be bringing an invalid lady to stay. She was not desperately ill they said.

On Mrs Chalkin's recommendation, the trio went to Dr Longrigg, a local practitioner. They wished him to visit a lady who would be arriving later in the day. They described her as 'extremely thin but healthy' and 'cleanly in her habits'.

They returned to Cudham and at 7 o'clock in the evening were bundling the dying Harriet, violently shaking, incapable of walking and constantly groaning, into a wagonette. Alice Rhodes joined the other three on the six-mile journey to Bromley station where they took a train to Penge. About nine o'clock the parties reached Mrs Chalkins' house. The landlady was horrified at what she saw. They had said the lady was not desperately ill but she was obviously so.

Lewis now decided to postpone the doctor's visit. The case is not as bad as all that,' he said. 'We'll wait till the morning.'

Calm enough, one has to say, for a man whose wife was on the point of death and whose baby boy had died the previous day.

Harriet Staunton died the next morning and Dr Longrigg signed a certificate giving the cause of death as 'apoplexy'. Lewis, anxious to wind matters up, made the funeral arrangements. It was to be properly carried out, he said, but not too expensive. Leaving the corpse with Mrs Chalkin and attempting to reassure her that Harriet had been a neighbour who had been in good health, the party returned to Cudham.

When Harriet's family heard of her death, her brother-in-law demanded a post-mortem. The inquest produced facts too horrifying to ignore. The nurse stated: 'I went to wash the body but it was so dirty I could not. The head was alive with lice . . . It was a sort of dirt on the body that appeared to have belonged to the bark of a tree and had been growing for a long time.'

Dr Longrigg withdrew his original certificate and now stated that Harriet had died from starvation, exacerbated by the journey to Penge. To this he added, neglect and exhaustion. 'The body was fearfully emaciated and filthily dirty all over,' he said. 'It weighed 5 stone 4 pounds. There was comparatively no breast.'

Inevitably Lewis and Patrick, Lizzie and Alice, were charged with murder. In Newgate, while awaiting trial at the Old Bailey – where it was thought that 'a more calm, dispassionate and unimpassioned judgement would be formed in their case than in Kent' – both women gave birth.

The trial report makes grim reading. It is a tale of casual indifference, gross callousness, frightening threats, occasional violence and calculated cruelty. Claire Brown in particular attested to Patrick's hitting Harriet as well as Tommy and his own wife.

The defence was based on the cause of death. Medical experts were called to assert that it was possible that Harriet had died from tubercular meningitis. While they did not condone the neglect, they would not accept Longrigg's assumption that this was the cause of death.

Unsurprisingly, the jury returned a verdict of guilty. The judge spoke of 'barbarity', of 'a poor innocent, outraged woman', and told the four prisoners that although they had not been charged with Tommy's death, 'I cannot help feeling satisfied within my own mind that you are guilty of contemplating and plotting and having brought about his death.' All four were sentenced to hang at Maidstone.

Then the campaigns began. Seven hundred doctors signed a document declaring a lack of conviction in the post-mortem conclusion. The *Lancet* insisted that before proving murder by starvation it was necessary to prove death by starvation and that had not been done. At Maidstone, the Association for the Abolition of Capital Punishment held a meeting, pleading for the lives of the four condemned. Letters, columns of them, appeared in all the national newspapers, many of them attacking the medical evidence.

The doubts cast upon the verdict influenced the home secretary. The powerful public appeals resulted in Alice Rhodes's immediate release, and the sentences of the others were reduced to life imprisonment. And still there were demands for a revision of sentences. Patrick died before release but Lizzie was freed in 1883 and Lewis, still proclaiming his innocence, left prison in 1897.

And still the questions remain. It is assumed that Patrick and his wife Lizzie, bearing much of the burden, were going to share Lewis's new-found fortune. But whose idea was it in the first place? And when was it first conjured up? How could these relatively well-educated, respectable people do what they did? Did no one ever have any pity for baby Tommy? Or for Harriet? What sort of people were these?

Busy, busy, always busy

Will you come into my parlour? said the spider…

Now, let's just get this straight. This woman did not go round the Richmond pubs selling jars of dripping made from human flesh. That's just saloon bar talk. It's macabre. Mrs Hayhoe, landlady at the Hole in the Wall in Park Road, apparently spread that tale but it's just not true. Yes, there was something about a black leather bag. She threw that away but what it was, there is no certainty. And yes, it has to be admitted. They never found the head.

Another thing to get straight is what to call her. We'll use the name they used in court. To us, she's Kate Webster. Neither Webb nor Gibbs nor Thomas, neither Shannon nor Lawless. Not Lawler either, though that was her real name.

So here comes Kate, on 4 March 1879, up to the door of the Porter family in Hammersmith. And she's a very grand lady now, silk dress, gold watch on a chain, rings, jewellery. Anne Porter didn't recognise her at first, didn't know her till she spoke in that strong County Wexford accent. She'd never seen her so splendidly arrayed before. She was never like that when she worked next door. She was just a skivvy then. Anne hadn't seen her for quite a while. How her fortunes had changed. Some people, eh?

Well, Kate tells Anne that she's just come over from Richmond by train because she wants a word with Mr Porter. He is at work at the moment, Anne says, but she invites Kate inside for a chat about old times. She tells her how Porter is doing well at the painting and decorating and the boy, young Bob, is with his father at the trade now. And Anne recalls Kate's kindness in those times past when she took such a loving interest in the Porter's little girl, now, alas, no longer with us. The chat goes on and they open the bottle that Kate has brought and later they send out for a half of gin because they both enjoy a tipple, especially Anne Porter who, truth to tell, sometimes enjoys it just a little too much.

Then Porter comes in and the boy with him. And Kate tells them all about the changes in her fortunes. She tells him she's widowed now and she's Mrs Thomas, living in Park Road in Richmond. At 2 Vine Cottages. It's semi-detached and very respectable. Anyway, an aunt has passed on leaving her quite comfortably off, what with the furniture and the house. But she's decided against staying and all she wants now is to go back to Ireland. Her father is ill and wants her back and you always have to help your ageing parents, don't you?

So, then, Kate puts her question, does Mr Porter, in his line of business, know of anyone who'll buy her furniture or who'll sell it for her? She doesn't know anybody in Richmond, she says, and these days you have to be so careful in these sorts of matters and Porter thinks he might just have the right feller in mind. He'll let her know.

Well, time flies and Kate has to be off. The Porter men, William and young Bob, say they'll walk part of the way back with her. After all, she's got that ever so heavy looking black leather bag. Good God, they probably say in a joking sort of way, 'Whatever have you got in there? You got the crown jewels or something? You'd think it had weights in it.' And they insist on carrying it because it's too much for a woman, even a big, strong, raw-boned young woman like Kate. So between them the two men carry the black bag.

They walk as far as the Hammersmith suspension bridge and call in for a noggin at the Oxford and Cambridge pub. Then Kate says she has to meet a friend in Barnes, just over the other side of the bridge. She won't be long, she says, and off she goes with the bag.

Twenty minutes later she's back, this time minus the bag. But now she's sporting five fine rings which the friend has given her. Actually, Kate tells them, they'd belonged to her sister who died and this friend has been keeping them for her.

But now it's getting dark and Kate asks if Mr Porter will allow young Bob to accompany her to Vine Cottages. You can't be too careful these days, she says. And Porter agrees, you can't be too careful this time of night. He says then they'll take the District line and Bob can be home in no time after he's done escort duty.

Up at Vine Cottages, perhaps at about 10 o'clock, Kate is in no hurry to dismiss the lad and at fifteen years of age, and after working with his father all day, he's in no hurry to go. Kate is pleased with life. Look at these, she says, showing him her passbooks from the Monarch Building Society and the Post Office Savings Bank. Both in her name, of course. Mrs Thomas.

There is one other thing, Kate says to the young feller. She'd be ever so grateful if he could give her a hand. She knows it's late but she has another box to take to a friend of hers. She'd really like to take it tonight. Would he mind? And, of course, he's willing to help her because she's an old friend of the family.

But it's a struggle all the way to the bridge at Richmond. It's about three quarters of a mile along Park Road and then along Mount Ararat Road before they cut down to the river. The white deal box, tied with rope, is quite small but it's really heavy even for the two of them. And it's made extra difficult because it has only one handle. But at last they're on the bridge and when they reach one of the recesses of the left hand side, on the Twickenham side of the river, Kate tells Bob to leave. 'You run back,' she says. 'I'll soon catch you up.'

And the lad runs back. He's swallowed Kate's tale that she's meeting her friend because he thinks that's the way adults behave at 11 o'clock at night. Or perhaps he tells himself, maybe that's how the Irish act. And as he runs back, he hears a splash in the water. A barge, he tells himself.

In a minute or two Kate's back with him. He's missed the last train, she tells him, but he can sleep at Vine Cottages tonight which is what he does. And it's all very chaste and the boy gets home safe, early the next morning, full of last night's adventures.

That same morning, at about 11 o'clock, Henry Wheatley, a coal porter, sees a small box bobbing on the water near Barnes Bridge, five miles or so from Richmond. He thinks his luck is in. He's not one to pass up what might be something valuable. So he fishes out the box. Inside are some parcels, each wrapped in brown paper. And there's what at first sight looks like meat. He wonders if it isn't some student prank but he calls the police just in case. At the mortuary, the incomplete remains of a woman are examined.

There is nothing to indicate who is lying on the slab. No one locally has been reported missing. What can be said is that one piece of flesh has been boiled. It's all been tightly packed in that little deal box. There is part of the chest, the heart, a piece of lung and some bits of a leg and an arm and a left foot. There is no head.

Now back to Kate. Perhaps here might be a good place to fill in some background. She was, in 1879, 30 years of age with a history of criminal offences. She'd done time in Ireland for larceny as well as in England where she'd served several prison terms, one of them in Newgate. She had done one four-year stretch and in 1875 had received 18 months at Surrey Assizes for 36 offences of theft. She had most recently been released after another 12 months imposed in February 1877.

Kate specialised in lodging house thefts, taking a room and then after a few days, disappearing with whatever took her fancy. Gaol-hardened by the time she showed up at Vine Cottages in January 1879, her sole aim was to carry out her usual con trick. Though she had an undoubtedly glib tongue, she was regularly found out in a short time. She really was not a good enough thief or liar though she was well enough practised.

Quite by chance Kate had been offered a job at Vine Cottages by Mrs Julia Martha Thomas, a tartar of a woman, who could never keep her servants. She was so demanding that whoever she employed upped and awayed as soon as they possibly could. And in January 1879 Mrs Thomas's cook had left her in the lurch. Desperate, she told a friend of her problem and the friend, who had once employed the young Irish woman called Kate Webster for a day or so, handed on the name. So on 27 January, after a cursory interview, Kate took up her appointment in the small semi that Mrs Thomas rented from Miss Ives, living next door at 1 Vine Cottages.

It was an ideal sort of place, Kate must have thought. The old lady – she was in her mid-50s – had elegant dresses and some fine jewellery. The furniture, too, was decent enough though the bulk of it belonged not to Miss Thomas but to her landlord.

Things appear not to have worked out from the start. Not that that would have worried Kate, who was indifferent to the opinions of any of her mistresses. But she was exasperated by Mrs Thomas, sitting there playing the piano, quite the lady, while she scrubbed floors, polished brasses, swilled the front step, cooked the meals. And there were two paying guests there for a couple of weeks. More work. Life's so unfair for a working woman. As for Mrs Thomas, she was apparently soon dissatisfied enough with her latest employee. Her diary for 28 February reads: 'Gave Katherine warning to leave.' If Kate was to make much out of this place, she would have to get a move on. But she was planning her departure prior to receiving notice.

On 25 February, Kate had visited a friend, Mary Durden, a straw-bonnet maker who lived in Kingston. Kate told her that her circumstances were due to change very soon. She was going to inherit property from an aunt in Birmingham. There was jewellery, too, she said, and a gold watch and chain. And furniture to sell. She'd be off to settle matters in a week or so. Her aunt was dying. By the time she got there, Kate expected she'd be dead.

Three days later she was back in Kingston, this time to Acre Street, where the father of Johnny, her five-year-old son, lived. Could she get her some sugar of lead? He could and did from a local chemist. But the poison was never used.

On 28 February Mrs Thomas's paying guests, Mrs Menhennick and her daughter from Raynes Park, left. The house was quieter. But from Sunday, 2 March, Kate was busier than ever. She had gone out on the Sunday afternoon and had too much to drink. When she came back she and Mrs Thomas had a row. From her demeanour that evening at the Presbyterian chapel, Mrs Thomas was evidently upset.

Kate's later confession describes what happened next. 'Upon her return from church, before her usual hour, she came in and went upstairs. I went up after her, and we had an argument which ripened into a quarrel, and in the height of my anger and rage, I threw her from the top of the stairs to the ground floor. She had a heavy fall. I felt that she was seriously injured and I became agitated at what had occurred, lost all control of myself and to prevent her from screaming or getting me into trouble, I caught her by the chest and in the struggle she was choked.'

The general view, however, is that Mrs Thomas was struck on the back of the head with a meat cleaver. After the trial, at an auction of household effects, a cleaver, claimed by the auctioneer to be the suspect weapon, went for five shillings.

The confession continues: 'I determined to do away with the body as best I could. I chopped the head from the body with the assistance of a meat saw which I used to cut through the flesh afterwards. I also used the meat saw and the carving knife to cut the body up with. I prepared the copper with water to boil the body to prevent identity, and as soon as I succeeded in cutting it up, I placed it on the copper and boiled it. I opened the stomach with the carving knife and burned up as much of the parts as I could.'

And so all through the night and into the next dawn Kate cuts, hacks, saws and slices. She struggles through bone, muscle, gristle and ligament. The copper is on and she boils flesh and clothing. Onto the kitchen fire she throws gut, sinew and bone. She scrubs floorboards, tables, knives, cupboards. Her hands, wrists and arms are crimson; her apron, her boots are spattered with reds and pinks, yellows and creams as she labours in the stench of it.

'I was greatly overcome, both from the horrible sight before me and the smell, and I failed several times in my strength and determination but was helped on by the Devil.'

Early on Monday, 3 March, Miss Ives at 1 Vine Cottages saw a light next door and at seven o'clock she heard the sound of washing and brushing in next door's scullery. Not that that was the only sound she'd heard. The night before there had been what she had taken for a chair falling over in the hall. By 11 o'clock in the morning the washing was out on the back garden line. So much early industry. And Miss Ives also remarked upon the smell!

There were other matters Kate had to deal with on that Monday. The coal man called with his bill. Mrs Thomas wasn't at home, Kate told him. Then Mrs Roberts, one of Mrs Thompson's friends, called round but Kate didn't answer the door.

On the Tuesday Miss Ives sent round her servant girl to tell Mrs Thomas that the men were coming to repair a leak. No need, Kate told her. It had just been the melting snow but there was nothing to repair.

It was the same day, 4 March, that Kate visited her old friends, the Porters. She had made a new friendship with Jack Church, a friend of the Porters and owner of the Rising Sun beer shop, just a few doors away from where the Porters lived. Over the next week he and Porter went to Vine Cottages several times to estimate the value of the furniture. It is hard to believe that Kate was other than a poor but a compulsive liar, for she told Church that she was going to Scotland to live with her father, a Glasgow solicitor. She told a similar story to another friend. How she kept the stories going with the Porters, who understood her to be going to live with her sick father in Ireland, is difficult to understand.

Church, who had some business acumen – there was least up to £500 in his bank account – was to allege that he thought Kate had a good business head on her shoulders. He took on the arrangements to have the furniture removed and sold elsewhere. He intended to buy some of the items himself and send off the rest to auction. Over several days he removed some of furniture – tablecloths, mats, glass from chandeliers, vases, carving knives and forks, candlesticks, plates and curtains – to the Rising Sun.

From 10 March, Church, a married man, called on Kate every day, taking her out for drinks, she wearing her satin-trimmed beefeater hat and the large ear rings that Church had bought her. The couple spent hours alone together in the house although she slept at nights at the Porters where little Johnny was now installed.

And nobody yet suspected that the remains washed up at Barnes Bridge had anything to do with Mrs Thomas. And nobody suggested that the ankle and foot found on an allotment manure-heap at Copthall in Twickenham on 10 March had anything to do with the former occupant of 2 Vine Cottages. Yes, busy though she was, Kate still had had time to make her way to Twickenham.

But if nobody suspected that Julia Thomas had been done away with, the neighbours had become increasingly curious. They had not seen her for days. And the servant and her behaviour were causing concern. Kate was in and out of the house every day with parcels, and nights she was never home. One day they saw her arm-in-arm with a man going into the house. Other times during the day, they had seen a man with a notebook going round the house and on at least one occasion they had heard the piano and singing. What on earth could Julia Thomas be thinking of?

If the neighbours were concerned they were not suspicious of anything like murder. Miss Ives had heard things, of course, but murder never entered her head. Porter who sold a set of false teeth for Kate – he got £6 for them – never suspected Kate of such a crime.

And friends who wrote and received no reply and others who called at the house equally unsuccessfully were no more than slightly puzzled, and through it all Kate Webster arranged the selling of her furniture; sees little Johnny at the Porters where he joins him at nights; meets Church for drinks and the passions of their short-lived love affair. Does she not think of the other awful matter? Doesn't she dream?

On Monday 17 March, with Church's help, Kate spent much of the day packing, getting things ready for the furniture removal. The next day Weston's two horse-drawn vans turned up at Vine Cottages. Then, right in the middle of all the bustle, out came Miss Ives calling out that they had no right to be taking the furniture from the house. It was hers, she said. 'And where is Mrs Thomas?' she demanded. If Porter and Church did not then realise that Kate had assumed her former employer's identity, they must at least have smelt a rat.

'You have deceived me,' Church told Kate. 'I'll have nothing to do with the goods. Put them back again.'

While the furniture was being carried back inside, Kate disappeared, finding a hansom cab round the corner to take her to the Rising Sun. Doubtless Mrs Church was surprised to see her. Wasn't she moving today? Wasn't her husband with Mr Porter at Vine Cottages? Kate spun a tale, for she was quick-witted in such circumstances. And could Mrs Church let her borrow a sovereign for some or other emergency Kate had dreamt up? Mrs Church, trusting soul, came up with the cash.

Off then to the Porters' house where doubtless Mrs Porter was equally amazed to see Kate. But no. Kay wanted Johnny with her. He had been with the Porters of the last ten days and now it appeared Kate wanted to take him to Richmond.

Then she was off again. But where? When they returned from Richmond, Porter and Church compared tales with their wives and could not satisfactorily explain what on earth was going on. Days later, however, a dress and hatbox which had been delivered by the removal men to the Church's house, helped solve the mystery.

On 21 March Mrs Church, inspecting the dress, found the letter in the pocket from Mrs Julia Thomas's friend. Mrs Manhenick of Raynes Park. Perhaps, Church and Porter agreed, she might be able to resolve the mystery. Off they went to Raynes Park. What they heard there was that the men's Mrs Thomas, a thirty-year-old, with a liking for gin and the mother of a little boy, was nothing like Mrs Menhennick's old friend. Clearly this was a police matter.

When the police searched the house they found hand bones hidden under the copper furnace and under the kitchen grate. In the copper, there was some fatty matter. There were smears of blood on the staircase, in the pantry and in the back bedroom. Evidently an attempt to boil and burn a body had been abandoned. There was a chopper and a razor in a cupboard.

A week or so later a lady who had announced herself as the widow of Captain J.W. Webster and the mother of four children, was arrested by detectives from London at Killaun in County Wexford. She was returned to Richmond and charged with murder.

In the course of a six-day trial Kate Webster tried unsuccessfully to pin responsibility on Jack Church, on Porter and on the father of her child. While it was a complex case, with fifty-three witnesses, confused with all the more or less innocent arrangements with the marvellously imprudent

Church and the astonishing naivety of the Porter family, Kate was condemned to death.

Thus on 29 July 1879, Kate Webster was hanged at Wandsworth. She had really gained little from her crime, which was not the rash act of temper which she claimed. She intended that Julia Thomas would die. But all she got out of it was £6 pounds for a set of false teeth; £11.10s which she found in the house; Church's £18 deposit on the furniture and only the promise of a balance of £60. And, of course, a few drinks on the way.

Jack

'Grand work the last job was . . .'

From a letter allegedly written by the Ripper dated 25 September, 1888.
It was forwarded to Scotland Yard by the Central News Agency.

It's always Jack, waiting in the shadows, flitting through our dreams, haunting the nightmare alleys of memory. Jack's the one who sets the standard against which all the rest are measured. Always Jack. Always with us.

Jack?

Jack who?

Jack the Ripper of course, that's who. Who else?

But first here's William Gull. Let's have a look at him. According to some experts, there was more to this eminently respectable old chap than meets the eye. Some, in fact, say that he was . . . But wait, let's have a look at him first.

On 3 February 1890 they brought Sir William Gull's body up by train from Liverpool Street station so that he could be buried at Thorpe-le-Soken, the Essex village where he had been born and where other members of his family were buried. Later in the day a special train conveyed members of the aristocracy, government ministers, the elite of the scientific and medical world in which he had achieved such distinction. Wreaths, including one from the Prince and Princess of Wales, decked the simple churchyard where crowds of locals gathered at the last resting place of one of Thorpe's most celebrated sons.

And he came from such humble beginnings, too, for Gull, the youngest of eight children, was born in 1816 on The Dove, his father's barge, at the time tied up at St Osyth Mill in the parish of St Leonard, Colchester. So there were no distinct privileges for this Essex lad. Yet despite such significant lack of advantage in an age in which birth connections meant so much, William Gull was to become one of the foremost medical men of his time. He was a fellow of the Royal Society, a fellow of the Royal College of Physicians and professor of physiology at Guys. In the course of his long career he attended to many eminent men and women and, in 1871, he was responsible for the treatment of the Prince of Wales during a threatening attack of typhus. In consequence of this he became a baronet. Sir William

Gull's final distinction was his appointment as physician-in-ordinary to Queen Victoria.

An enviable career, one must admit. The rise from such beginnings can command nothing but admiration and respect and yet there were rumours, stories relating to events in his last years which clung to Gull's reputation.

Indeed, they attached to Gull up to quite recent times at Thorpe-le-Soken and in the world at large for that matter.

For example, some have said that Gull was never buried on that early February day. Some hinted that another

man's body had been interred. Others have claimed that nothing but a coffin full of stones went into the ground while Gull himself, under an assumed name, was confined in some private madhouse. Could it be so? Could such a tortuous trick have been played out. But by whom? And why?

Writer Stephen Knight, visiting the churchyard in the 1970s, spoke to the verger who commented: 'This is a large grave, about twelve feet by nine and too large to be for two people (Gull and his wife). Some say more than two are buried here. It's big enough for three, that grave.' The verger went on to tell Knight, 'Burial places for two aren't normally that big. Of course, it's possible that somebody else is buried there without anybody knowing who.'

A third body in the grave? There is no record of anyone but Gull and his wife in that plot.

Other researchers have come across a strongly held belief in Thorpe-le-Soken that whoever was buried in February 1890, it was not Sir William Gull. Many believed that it was several years later that he was put into the grave in circumstances of great secrecy.

Mysteries, then. Rumours lingering so many years after the man's supposed burial.

The will, for example. It was, very naturally, probated in 1890 but why, when nothing seems to have changed, was it probated a second time in 1897? Is that when Gull really died? Had he been, as some have suggested, locked away insane all those years?

And another curious fact – Gull's death certificate was signed by his son-in-law, Dr Theodore Dyke Acland. While not illegal, it was unusual for a relative to sign such a document. After all when Gull died – when he is alleged to have died – there were other medical men present.

But the real mystery which attaches to Sir William Gull is something more significant than an important figure in the world of medicine being placed in a Victorian insane asylum.

In April 1895 the *Chicago Sunday Times-Herald* ran a story about the mystic Robert James Lees, who claimed to have taken a detective to a house in London where a distinguished physician had lived. This physician, Lees claimed, had been placed in an insane asylum under the name of Thomas Mason. His death had been announced and a fake funeral held.

And this subterfuge was to cover up the identity and fate of the serial killer known variously as Leather Apron, the Whitechapel Murderer or, most famously of all, as Jack the Ripper. As some have asserted, presumably have been asserting since 1895, Sir William Gull was that man.

There has been great speculation down the years about Jack's identity. Much of the early evidence, taken in times when record-keeping was less fastidious than now, has been lost. Some documents were taken as souvenirs; others were destroyed when the case was closed in 1892 and it was assumed that it would never be resolved. The Blitz took care of other written evidence. Indeed, it is not totally unfair to suggest that much of what we 'know' about the Ripper comes from the researches and speculations of more recent days. But some of these researchers write about material being deliberately destroyed or hidden. What was so secret about Jack?

Jack was the first serial killer to catch the public imagination, the first to be written up in the newspapers, especially *The Times* and the *Daily Telegraph*, and written with such relish that he came to find a lasting place in our national mythology. Yet it is not really certain how many women he slew. Estimates vary between four and nine, but five is the generally accepted figure, all done to death in the restricted area of Whitechapel, Spitalfields, Aldgate and the City of London between the late summer and late autumn of 1888, August to November, just a few short weeks to make his name, to become, in fact, one of the immortals.

Forensic evidence indicates that all of the victims were strangled standing, facing a man they took to be a client. They were then lowered to the ground and Jack's work began. He now cut their throats, taking his knife from the right-hand side. The extensive and ferocious mutilations of the abdomen of several of the women were also from the right. It seems that by operating in this way with his victims on the ground, he had less chance of bloodying himself. Does this suggest some awareness of surgery?

Like many serial killers Jack took trophies too. On one occasion it was a kidney, cut out unusually enough from the front though without causing damage to any other organs. On another occasion he removed the sexual organs with one bold, confident stroke.

Imagine, only one of his five acknowledged killings was made inside a house. The others were in yards, in dark alleyways, out in the open, at dead of night.

Jack's surgery was invariably hurried for fear of his being caught. It took place in poor light. While at the time there was some disagreement about his surgical skills, it is now generally accepted that here was a man of some considerable skill going about his work in the dark.

Gull?

Well, Sir Melville McNaughton, chief constable in 1894, never even considered Gull to be a suspect in a confidential report on the unsolved crimes. But then what if the Ripper's identity was known to a select band of people? What if there were considered to be pressing reasons to protect the Ripper? What if even McNaughton was in some kind of plot to conceal the identity of the murderer? This is certainly a highly popular view, the romantic tale of a conspiracy which reached and touched the highest in the land.

Stephen King's *Jack the Ripper: The Final Solution*, published in 1978, propounds this theory. He claims that Joseph Sickert, son of the Victorian painter, Walter Sickert, told him the outline of the story and that, having researched it thoroughly, accepted broadly what he had been told. Melvin Fairclough's gripping *The Ripper and the Royals*, which came out in 1991, covers even more of this ground.

The story involved Prince Albert Victor, the Duke of Clarence, who was himself at one time a likely candidate in some researchers' analyses as the Ripper. But the evidence clears the Duke. The involvement of Eddy, as he was familiarly known, was, according to Knight and Fairclough, nevertheless real. Joseph Sickert explained to them, at various times, that the Prince and

Sickert's father used regularly to frequent the East End of London. The bisexual Prince, acting incognito, enjoyed himself in the shadier parts of town. But then, the story goes, he met Annie Crook, fell in love with her, married her secretly, and there was a baby, Alice Margaret. Naturally this arrangement was kept secret for how could a prince of the realm, son of the heir to the throne, grandson of Victoria, possibly marry a commoner? And a Catholic at that.

And when the news ultimately leaked to Queen Victoria she insisted that action be taken. She called on her prime minister, Lord Salisbury.

'Action, ma'am, but what action?' he might have said. But again, according to the Sickert/Knight/Fairclough account, that was left to him to decide.

Joseph Sickert told Knight how the house in Cleveland Street where Eddy and Annie and their baby were installed was suddenly raided. Eddy was taken away in one cab, the bewildered Annie in another to begin a tragic and awful downward descent. The baby, Alice Margaret, was smuggled away to the care of nuns by nursemaid, Mary Kelly.

The story then swings onto Mary Kelly, who herself in turn goes into a downward spiral of drink and prostitution. And maudlin Mary, unable in drink to keep the information to herself, tells her friends all about the Duke and his wife and the baby and the raid. And her friends, tut-tutting, say how dreadful it is and how immoral and shouldn't something be done about it. They're all on the game but artless enough, and they think the government ought to fork out a few quid because it's awful what they have done. And all this chatter, chatter, chatter doesn't do any good to anybody. And it has to be stopped.

So the great government conspiracy comes into operation again. Having saved Eddy from his worst self and having silenced Annie by having Gull perform operations on her brain, they are now confronted by these dreadful prostitutes demanding cash.

So Jack is no solitary madman stalking prostitutes. He is an agent of the government, protecting the security of the State and the good name of the royal family. The head of the conspiracy is Lord Randolph Churchill. But the workman, the butcher, is Gull, that staunch servant of the Crown, who goes out at night to his work, sitting in a coach driven by John Netley, who used to take Eddy out on his East End jaunts. And inside the coach with Gull is Eddy's boon companion Walter Sickert, who will act as look-out whenever one of these loud-mouthed women is being attended to.

They are, all of them, these women, common prostitutes, given to drink and for most of their days destitute. They are in common lodging houses or workhouses or from time to time, driven by their inevitable health problems, in infirmaries. All of them, save the last victim, are in their mid-forties.

On the last day of August, Mary Ann Nicholls meets Jack in a narrow, cobbled street and is only, according to the police report, 'slightly mutilated.' Here, less than a fortnight later, 'Dark Annie' Chapman encounters him and is left with some of her entrails round her neck. Catherine Eddowes and 'Long Liz' Stride meet their end on the same day, 30 September. And 25-year -old 'Ginger', Mary Jane Kelly, is the last victim. She lets him into her squalid little room and she most of all suffers the most ghastly mutilation.

Remember her? Mary Jane Kelly? She was the nursemaid of little Alice Margaret and so now, with the last of the potential blackmailers done to death, Jack is able to retire, his duty to the Crown, to his nation, now complete. Gull can return to respectability. Only a few weeks of the dying year, that's all it has taken. In that time the women are dispatched and 'girls' can resume a normal life. Annie, increasingly insane, survives in poverty for the next thirty years.

At least that is a compelling and persuasive version of the famous tale, debunked by many serious Ripperologists but popular with those who enjoy late-flowering Gothic horror laced with conspiracy theory.

But there are questions. There are, for instance, several to be asked about Sir William Gull.

The first is, if you wished to hire an assassin would you choose a man whose whole life had been eminently respectable? Would you expect him to act in this ultimately depraved manner? Who would you think of as the ideal man to select for this hazardous task? A man 70 years of age? And even if he fitted in all other respects, wasn't the man who had recently given up his medical practice after suffering a stroke entirely unsuited to such work?

Gull's story certainly has some odd features. The will, for example; the site of the grave; the possibility even that he did not die in 1890 but was committed to an asylum: all these seem to be worthy of enquiry. But none of it really adds up to his being more than an eminent medical man. It certainly does not make him a convincing or suitable candidate for the world's best-known serial killer.

One of the most distinguished of those who lie in the graveyard at Thorpe-le-Soken really does seem to have been ill-treated by posterity but does not deserve so ill a reputation. But he does, nevertheless, leave some interesting questions.

So, whodunnit? We shall never know but he must seriously consider others whose names occupied the time of so many police officers and particularly Montague John Druitt, Walter Sickert, Thomas Cutbush and Seweryn Klosowski aka George Chapman.

But they're for another day.